You Will Live and Not Die

FORCED HAND

A Book of Transformation

James Washington, Jr.

Published by
Hadassah's Crown Publishing, LLC 634
NE Main St #1263
Simpsonville, SC 29681

Library of Congress Catalog Number: 2022915364

ISBN: 978-1-950894-88-8

Printed in the United States

This book is dedicated to the spiritually and naturally:

- Incarcerated

- Previously Incarcerated

- Disabled Veteran

- Poor/Homeless

- People of a wayward lifestyle

- The Church

These seven demographics of individuals are much more than the people I was called to deliver a word to from the Lord. The Lord sent me to these specific people in these last days because of my testimony and the blood of the Lamb that loved and saved me. I also wholeheartedly and empathetically share their pain, experiences, and doubts as I questioned God's unique plans and purposes for my life. Now the Lord uses my life experiences to speak into theirs. After years of being humbled in my body, spirit, heart, and soul, sticking to the process, I was finally in a position where I could be used to do my Father in heavens' will and serve my Lord and Savior Christ Jesus with this written testimony. Praying daily for help, grace, and mercy to lean not on my own understanding but to learn a little more each day that He kept my eyes open and breath in my lungs to trust the Lord in all my ways is the foundation and my written testimony to all who receive this word.

"If you love them like you say you do, write the books," is my calling. This book is dedicated to the numerous brothers and sisters in my Air Force family and extended family in which I died in my former ways to make this life transition a reality. John Stevenson & family, Lisa Mickens & family, Marilyn Smith & family, Greg Torry & family, Lafayette Charleston & family, LaTonya Davis & family, Marichal Hubbard & family, Britt English & family, Marcellus Saunders & family, Roger Lantry & family, Doc Porter & family, Don Singleton & family, Mr. Ed, and Miss Ingy. I died to my old life's thoughts, attitudes, and behaviors and was reborn in my spirit by the word that cleansed me to complete this assignment. I didn't stop communicating with all of you because I didn't love you, but because I love you dearly and share this message that you will live and not die forced hand. I miss you all, and I have continued to pray for you and your families throughout our time apart.

This book is dedicated to my immediate family, my deceased father and mother, James and Christine Washington. Rest in peace, family; I love you both. To my brother Joe & family, sister Marie, nieces Tina, Nique, Cora, Sha'Kira, Re'naia, Aaliyah, Ivanna, nephew Money, Fred, and Chicago. This book is dedicated to my late cousin Cora Henderson who supported me in the spirit until the Lord saw fit to bring her home in rest. God rest you, cousin.

Finally, this book is dedicated to my late wife, Laura L. Washington, whose recent passing, the Lord used to show me His great love, not my own. I couldn't help you or save you, but Jesus has prepared a home for you, not made of hands. My regret is I never got to ask you the questions, and you never got an opportunity to read the books you watched me year after year pursue; three questions and two books I am supposed to share with the world that I never had a chance to share with you.

Through this loss, the Lord created in me a new heart and a new sense of urgency that no one He sent me to witness will leave this world devoid of what the Lord has to say in this season through me, His servant, and the works of my hand. Love you, and may you rest in peace, Laura L. Washington.

You Will Live and Not Die FORCED HAND

CONTENTS

INTRODUCTION

"The right hand of the Lord is exalted; The right hand of the Lord does valiantly. I shall not die, but live, and declare the works of the Lord. The Lord has chastened me severely, but He has not given me over to death," (Psalms 118:16-18 NKJV). "Do not marvel at this; for the hour is coming in which all who are in the graves will hear His voice and come forth those who have done good, to the resurrection of life, and those who have done evil, to the resurrection of condemnation," (John 5:28-29). "And these will go away into everlasting punishment, but the righteous into eternal life," (Matthew 25:46).

How different would your life be if someone told you and you genuinely believed in your heart that there is a book in heaven with your name written on it? What if someone told you this book in heaven has your entire life story and contains the plans and purposes God alone created you to do on the earth? (Psalms 139:16). On the other hand, this book also includes every secret thing you ever thought, wanted to do, did do, and every good thing you could have done but chose not to do from birth to death (Revelation 20:12). What if that same person told you that you could be judged with specific eternal ramifications for every derogatory comment and every sinful thing you did not repent of during your lifetime? This truth could very well be why the Bible tells us there is none righteous, no not one (Romans 3:10). No one on this earth has ever sustained pure thoughts, attitudes, and motives all the days of their life except One Person. With this train of thought, the believer, and the unbeliever alike, any logical person can perceive why the Bible is the most important book in the world, whether you believe in it or choose not to believe (Bible IQ). No book has come close to diagnosing man's predisposition, world history, and future prophecy with one hundred percent accuracy. The fact remains that one day you and that mortal body (we coin EARTH suit) will die. And again, only One Person has ever returned from death and the grave to tell us what happens next. This book is written to HELP people not to fail an open book test containing severe, dangerous, and eternal consequences to their spirit and soul. The title of this book aims to inspire HOPE for the future to anyone willing to receive this word of the gospel to choose right with God, and life eternal, which is the heart of God for all His created people (Deuteronomy 30:19). Everything, though created by God, is not acceptable to God, or there would be no need for the Bible or the law. While researching for this work, I found a considerable portion of my days shaking my head, looking around in disbelief, checking off the boxes, and watching this world unravel right before my very eyes. The grace of God over my life allows me to see things from a perspective that many cannot because before I gave my life to Christ and was reborn of His water and the Spirit, I was once the people I look at today. But God! God had his tender, loving, precious mercy over me and saved my life. He had a job for me. He told me while having one foot in the grave and one out, I would live and not die. But the understanding was concise when He emphasized that He was not saving me for my benefit only but also for all who would receive this work. He said, "If you love them like you say you do, write the books." I didn't know what "write the books" meant then, but I am beginning to understand now. I have lived a miraculous and grace-filled life from birth to this very day, and I write to you from a position of humbleness, gratefulness, obedience, and thankfulness for all the Lord has done for my loved ones and me.

Listen, I get it; all we need is one more person who claims that he hears from the Lord and that people should believe what he says. Honestly, I get it, and you would be right; many people these days who claim to hear from the Lord don't. So why should you listen to Bro Wash? Four reasons: first, if anyone says that they have heard from the Lord through the Holy Spirit but cannot tell you the four voices that occupy their minds be wary. A person who genuinely hears from the Lord must distinguish between his flesh, this world, the enemy, and the will of God to profess its validity. Second, be very skeptical if a person has no fear of God, no humility, and does not communicate the truth in love. Also, if the word he speaks is only peace to you in this age while this world is spiraling quickly toward its judgment, slow down. Third, this is my assignment in this EARTH suit by the grace of God; nothing on my own entitles me in any way other than to be a sinner saved by His amazing grace for His service. The Lord saved me to proclaim this message of the Kingdom of God on earth. Nothing about this writing glorifies me. This writing only glorifies our Heavenly Father in Christ Jesus and the power of the Holy Spirit for the season of His Church that He said the gates of hell would not prevail against them (Mark 16:18). The Bible says but seek first the Kingdom of God and His righteousness, and all these things shall be added to you (Matthew 6:33). I didn't wake up one day and say to myself, "I'm going to recruit souls for the Kingdom of God," for the rest of my life, and shut myself up in a room for five years. I didn't even know what the Kingdom of God was then. No, only God foreknows, predestines, calls, justifies, and glorifies his servants for His purposes before the foundations of the earth (Romans 8:28-31). Everything in my life this far has brought me here by His right Hand, not my own, and with life experiences too numerous to list, from birth to this day. The shortlist is as follows:

1. I was born to a woman who was not even supposed to have kids.

2. I should have drowned after being pushed into a river and unable to swim.

3. After eighteen years, I am still in the land of the living with a now undetectable but previously undiagnosable bleeding disorder and numerous core morbidities presently controlled.

4. I experienced salvation and deliverance from alcohol, depression, sexual immorality, immoral living, and dangerously no fear of God.

These very things the hand of the Lord has shown His abundant grace and mercy to me so that I can encourage others of not what you can't do, but what some people won't do because of the things we will discuss in the upcoming chapters. I didn't validate myself or get "spiritual" reading the Bible and coin my life to write a book; quite the opposite, I found myself living a life already written in the Holy Scriptures (1 Corinthians 6:1). All this, being called out in my spirit to complete this work with no previous experience and directed to "write what I see" from a seat and world view designed perfectly to my experiences that glorify God in Christ Jesus in service. In this book, the hand of the Lord represents these 12 facets:

1. The grace of God (Isaiah 66:2)

2. The mercy of God (Isaiah 65:2)

3. The love of God (Psalms 145:16)

4. The peace of God (Psalms 31:15)

5. The righteousness of God (Acts 5:31)

6. The Holiness of God (Psalms 28:5)

7. The truth of God (Acts 11:21)

8. The sovereignty of God (1 Chronicles 29:12)

9. The power of God (Daniel 4:35)

10. The will of God (Job 12:10)

11. The hand of the Lord represents the blessings of God for those who diligently seek Him and His face (Psalms 92:4)

12. Finally, the flip side of the blessings is the wrath of God for those who are his enemy, who rebel and disobey his commands (Jeremiah 15:6). Not many people have documented evidence (pictures, notes, receipts, witnesses, testimonies of deliverance) of the hand of the Lord on

their lives. And if you're not aware of its importance in these last days, you will have no rest, no peace, and most importantly, no power to thwart the constant attacks of the enemies against your spirit and soul. So, my brother or sister, if you knew none of this and you would like to know more, you should keep reading this book written by someone that was sent (Matthew 13:52) and writes by example from God's grace, mercy, and patience.

We, the saved, called, and chosen of God, have a gift, assignment, or something God placed inside us through the grace of Christ Jesus by faith to do as members of His church (2 Timothy 1:9-10). My mission in the church body is to write the vision to recruit souls through the doctrine of the Kingdom of God in these last days. I am not a pastor, preacher, or evangelist. Those occupations have more than enough participants. In the Bible, I would be considered a scribe. My vocation is Human Resource Management (interpreting company policy, procedures, compliance, training, development, and benefits), which I do for the Kingdom of God. The Lord Jesus said, "Then He said to them, 'Therefore every scribe instructed concerning the Kingdom of Heaven is like a householder who brings out of his treasure things new and old,'" (Matthew 13:52). Then the Bible says in the Book of Mark, one of the scribes who perceived that Jesus had answered all questions well asked Him of the greatest commandment of all; the Bible says, "So the scribe said to Him, 'Well said, Teacher. You have spoken the truth, for there is one God, and there is no other but He. And to love Him with all the heart, with all the understanding, with all the soul, and with all the strength, and to love one's neighbor as oneself, is more than all the whole burnt offerings and sacrifices.' Now when Jesus saw that he answered wisely, He said to him, 'You are not far from the Kingdom of God,'" (Mark 12:32-34).

Five is the number of grace. The Lord gave me three questions and two books to share, specifically to the seven demographics I previously mentioned: the incarcerated, previously incarcerated, disabled veterans, poor, homeless, people of a wayward lifestyle, and the church.

My assignment in these last days is as follows:

Question one: In John 11:25, the Bible says Jesus said to her, "I am the resurrection and the life. He who believes in Me, though he may die, he shall live. And whoever lives and believes in Me shall never die. Do you believe this?" I pose this question to the seven demographics, leading to this first book's title.

- The name of this first book is entitled *You Will Live*

& Not Die: Forced Hand. This book addresses the first question from the natural perspective for those who doubt life after death, but even more so the spiritual ramifications that suggest the inevitability of life "somewhere" and judgment after the mortal death of this fleshly body. The subheading "*Forced Hand*" introduces the following question in my assignment.

Question two: Do you know what the hand of the Lord represents throughout the Bible, in your life, upon this nation and world in these last days? As we listed above, ten attributes of the hand of the Lord produce one of two consequences concerning where you spend your life after mortal death. The hand of the Lord is of the utmost importance to assess, understand, and differentiate what is and what is not the will of the Lord for this lost generation. Those who have a proper understanding of the hand of the Lord can teach others to prepare for the chaos and deception that is already here and working in this world and the church.

Question three: Do you know what is in your book? This work talks about three books you must be intimately familiar with in these last days. The Little Book is your Bible; this book gives instruction, guidance, warnings, and prophecy that guides you through mortal life, preparing you for life eternal. The second is Your Book. There is an adage, "my life is an open book," yet people have no idea how accurate this saying is. You are going through a series of tests documented throughout your life to determine where you will spend your eternity. Every day you breathe, you can edit your book positively through good works, repentance, prayer, and good biblical knowledge and wisdom. Or you can negatively impact your book and, subsequently, your eternal standing through not knowing God, not believing, and trusting in His Son alone, and refusing to repent of your sins. If your book is positive and acceptable, it leads to the second book and final assignment I have in this mortal body.

- The second and final book is entitled, *You Shall Live & Not Die: The Covenant.* This book differentiates between the future tense verb "will" live in the first book and the word "shall" live that this work uses to describe the covenantal agreement between the children of God, the True Believers, and the good plans God has for them. The book also addresses, as this book also does, what is in store for the unbelieving, cowardly, murderers, sexually immoral, abominable, idolaters, and all liars (Revelation 21:8). This second book contains more principles, strategies, training, development, and testing resources and materials to aid and prepare the seven demographics in the last days for the natural and spiritual warfare they will incur.

This book is written as simply as possible in the vernacular of this generation. It aims to lead people to the only viable and acceptable narrow road to salvation, our Lord and Savior, Christ Jesus alone. Filled and motivated through God's grace, His infallible word, and His hand on my life are precepts and principles of the Kingdom of God to HELP individuals navigate this life during these deceptive times and foster HOP^{2}E^2 in these last days for whosoever wills. HELP is an acronym meaning Honoring Every Life Precious, which is the heart of God for everything He has created that contains breath. This is important in a world where people do not value the life of fetuses, animals, or the environment. I am prayerful this work will give some another perspective from the hand of God.

HOP^{2}E^2 is an acronym meaning: Helping Others Prepare and Prevail by Exposure and Example.

Helping Others involves loving everyone with the faithfulness and gentleness the Holy Spirit has deposited and works inside of me to live and write this vision for this generation to successfully:

• Empty false and unprofitable teachings and behaviors

- Expose this generation to this message of the Kingdom of God

- Envision the promises of God for those who endure to the end (Matthew 10:22)

- And encourage the naturally and spiritually incarcerated, previously incarcerated, disabled veterans, poor, homeless, the church, and people of a wayward lifestyle.

Prepare. There are four spiritual wars the saints of this generation are fighting as we speak and losing horrifically.

- The Days of Noah Part II: The Reign of Fire (1 Peter 3:20)

- Sodom and Gomorrah: The Next Chapter (Jude 1:7)

- The Teachings of Balaam: The 21st Century Apostasy (Revelation 2:14)

- Babylon 7 DEFCON II: The Transition from the "Great I AM" to "AI Technology" (Daniel 12:4)

Prevail as one mind in the body of the church against the gates of hell (Matthew 16:18) by

- Example (1 Corinthians 3:13-15)

- Exposure to the Kingdom of God (Matthew 6:33)

As I look back over my life and see the design and orchestration of how the Lord kept, delivered, and saved me, I can do nothing but fall on my knees with gratefulness and thanksgiving. By grace through faith, the Lord has given me the ability, heart, and anointing to accomplish this good work. The capabilities include the training, resources, availability, isolation, and heart He started and will finish through this work through the patience of God! Specifically, the heart the Lord gave me is my family, friends, and all the people I have learned from and interacted with worldwide. The Lord expressly said, "If you love them like you say you do, write the books." What does that even mean? Glad you asked! Of the nine years it has taken me to complete this first book, if someone had asked me what that meant up until 24 April 2022, I would have given them an incorrect answer through ignorance of what I understood about my calling included. Through the Holy Spirit's help by the Word of God I received through the ministry of Pastor Darius Daniels, I was much better but still only had a partial understanding. It was not until the Lord set a Fire $A^2L^2AR^4M^3$ off in my life at the end of 2022 that I began to get complete clarity.

The Bible uses fire as a metaphor for judgment (Amos 7:4) and a refining tool (Zechariah 13:9). By His will, the Lord assessed that I must experience judgment and refining to prepare me for what He assigned me to complete. A few months after the sermon by Dr. Daniels, I received a message in my spirit that I would lose some things in 2022, having seven months remaining. Starting on 28 June and spiraling quickly after that: I lost my car, dealt with injuries, incurred debt, lost some friends and classmates, and on 8 November, I lost a piece of me; my ex-wife unexpectedly lost her life. The totality of everything I endured in the summer of 2022 was the fire, but the passing of my wife set off the $A^2L^2AR^4M^3$.

The acrostic meaning of $A^2L^2AR^4M^3$ is as follows:

Adversity and Affliction in 2022 after suffering a

Loss showed me the Love of God, not my own, who then made me

Accountable despite my feelings of

Regret and Remorse, He Restored me, Redeeming the time creating a new

Mission and Ministry in Me that are fueled by the urgency to not fail another by not asking them three simple questions, to which I, in Christ Jesus, by the power and knowledge of the Holy Spirit, have the answers.

Our emotions and feelings often lead us on paths of self-righteousness, as if we know what people need based on our limited experiences, especially those close to us. We tend to want to teach and lead them once we have earnestly tasted the Lord's goodness and mercy. The truth is, I didn't even know what I needed, much less other people, until I went through numerous processes, testing, and chastening from the Lord. Love is causing no harm to another by actions, deeds, or words (Romans 13:10). I didn't love people like I said because I know things people need to know that are still inside my head, helping no one. The Lord told me to write everything He shows me, not give my family, friends, and people I interact with lectures, validating myself, or keep making excuses on where the books are He said to write. Obedience is the key to everything, exactly as the Prophet Samuel explained to King Saul in his day (1 Samuel 15:22). There is only one way to do this work, and that's "all in." Just like God knew where Adam was in the garden, God knew it would never be by my profession of love that this work gets done. It's not my love for myself or others that has gotten me this far, but His love for us that He kept extending and showing in His grace toward me as an example of His faithfulness and love toward us all. Through the Kingdom of God in whom I serve, I humbly receive the anointing, which gives the keys to all knowledge, wisdom, and understanding according to the grace and faith our Lord and Savior Christ Jesus alone has seen fit to instill in me (Ephesians 4:7). These experiences have prepared me with the life lessons necessary to write these books from a ministering, holistic, sympathetic, and empathetic point of view. What I do now until the Lord calls me home is complete the good works written for me before the foundations of the earth. You will live and not die, my brothers and sisters, forced hand.

My Prayer

These are words You put in my mouth, Lord, and told me to eat. These are the words You wrote on my heart Lord, my God in Christ Jesus, and the power of His Holy Spirit to relay to whosoever will receive it. These books are the work of my hands, my Lord, and I pray that my prayers shall be acceptable to You. I believe the Lord I serve will accept and bless the works of my hands if I keep my faith in Him alone. Amen

The Bible says to you has been given to know the mysteries of the Kingdom of God, but to the rest, it is shown in parables that seeing they do not see and hearing they do not hear (Luke 8:10). This book and ministry are founded on this message of the Kingdom of God. The Kingdom of God is the governing authority through and in the Holy Spirit in this age until the physically resurrected Christ Jesus returns to take His throne. Our Lord Jesus said, "the law and the prophets were until John; since that time, the Kingdom of God has been preached, and everyone is pressing into it," (Luke 16:16). John the Baptist first proclaimed the Kingdom of Heaven, the physical rulership of Christ Jesus in his wilderness ministry (Matthew 3:2). This announcement was shortly fulfilled when Christ Jesus was baptized (Matthew 3:16-17) and tempted by Satan (Matthew 4:1), then Christ Jesus proceeded to assume His ministry and preach, "Repent for the Kingdom of Heaven is at hand" (Matthew 4:17). The Bible gives us the clues of the succession of the authority when it specifies,

- The authority of the law and prophets until John (Matthew 3:2)

- John the Baptist succeeding to The Kingdom of Heaven (Matthew 11:12)

- I (John) must decrease, and He (Jesus) must increase (Matthew 3:30)

- Jesus announces that time is fulfilled, and the Kingdom of God is at hand (Mark 1:15)

- The Kingdom of Heaven succeeding to the Kingdom of God (Mark 1:15)

- The Kingdom of God reigns until Lord Jesus returns, reconciling the authority of heaven and earth to Himself (Matthew 28:18, Mark 14:25)

This God-ordained title of this book is essentially the bottom line of the gospel message expressing the good news that eternal life is available for those who believe and are baptized

(Mark 16:16). The first clause, "You Will Live & Not Die," depicts all humanity, three parts, body mortal, perishing; soul and Spirit belonging to God (Ezekiel 18:4) and will return to God, the Immortal and Eternal God Jehovah. "Forced Hand" culminates the relationship-centered reality between all humanity, including everything made called the "created" and God, "The Creator." This eternal relationship is explored throughout the book on the premise that the earthly body will die once, then judgment (Hebrews 9:27), but your soul and spirit will live forever, dependent upon your life choices (Joshua 24:15).

This book is divided into four areas of my vocation as a Kingdom recruiter: to expose, empty, envision the promise, and encourage whosoever receives this word.

Expose: In the sense that once you have experienced anything in life, you cannot be unexposed except through death.

Empty: The Bible says you can't put new wine into old wineskins because the acidity of the fresh wine will eat through the used wine bag (Matthew 9:17). Likewise, it does not benefit you to implement new ideas into an old mindset. The objective is to persuade the reader through the Holy Spirit to give up any invalid, incomplete thoughts, attitudes, and behaviors to the standard of mercy and grace through repentance offered to whosoever wills in the Kingdom of God.

Envision: This is the reception of what God is saying to you, specifically in this season, through His revealed Word and the promises associated with the Word of God.

Encourage: The goal is for "whosoever wills" reading this material that, like me, earnestly wants to understand the truth in these last days with sound principles that ultimately plant HOP^2E^2 while building disciples for the Kingdom of God. It is also to encourage readers to reflect on the Kingdom of God from an HR-centered perspective, these three areas are where we will be focusing our attention:

Rooting Out False Visions and Teachings

Tearing Down Divinations and Overthrowing Futility

Destroying Deceptions of One's Mind

These previous statements pave the way for the thesis and introduction of this message of the Kingdom of God.

The mention of the Kingdom message, as it was in Jesus's day, is still as mysterious as it is today. The Kingdom sticker of approval is applied everywhere, from children to individual and corporate platforms. I am not exactly sure how I became intrigued with the word "Kingdom," but I know it goes back farther than I can remember. The official definition of the

Kingdom of God for this work is **"God's accepted and man's approved spiritual will of joy, peace, and righteousness in the Holy Spirit reflected through His church on the earth, which gives power; to influence whosoever will's character, (thoughts, attitudes, and behaviors) in service to Christ Jesus.**

The Bible says, and on this one thing, most Christians can agree that the Kingdom of God is the key to all things in this season (Matthew 6:33). I hope this work makes you excited to learn more. Understanding the Kingdom of God will help you start to prioritize your life decisions and prayerfully discover your purpose. Next, we pray that this book refocuses you on building a relationship with Christ Jesus rather than the traditions and religion of man through sound biblical doctrine influenced by this message of the Kingdom. Even if you are not a believer, the average person probably already knows that you are not condemned for anything you did in your past as a True Believer. The cross and the innocent blood of Christ Jesus, who died for the entire world's sins, satisfied this enormous debt (John 3:16). You may have even read those Believers are covered from anything they do in their future because they have been sealed with the Holy Spirit unto redemption (Ephesians 4:30). But did you know that True Believers are even covered from the things they do right now because of the Word of God that washes and cleanses us daily (John 15:3)? Yes, that's right; you are not condemned for what you did, what you will do in the future, or even what you are doing right now. So, what will send you to hell and condemnation? This book, *You Will Live & Not Die: Forced Hand*, will explore these truths. God has done everything possible for you and me to have eternal life, even at the expense of sacrificing His One and only Son as propitiation and a substitute for our sinful lives. This book challenges the intellect of those who profess to be knowledgeable yet play Russian roulette with their spirit and souls, which are the only things known to be eternal by their professed understanding.

Everything that you need to know about "good success" (Joshua 1:8) now and in the next life is in one book called the "Holy Scriptures," or Bible, in which all this information is predicated, based, and given to me and all witnesses to Jesus Christ through the Holy Spirit.

There is not one person besides Christ Jesus who has lived on this earth and not pondered what the end of this life will behold. The notion that You Will Live and Not Die: Forced Hand if for no other reason still should make one envision possibilities. This work suggests whether you choose to live with Jesus in eternity or with the enemy in the SPA (Satan's

Permanent Abode) of brimstone and fire, my friend, is totally and definitively up to you. The assignment given to me is to write the books that point to the One who is called Faithful and True, and in righteousness, He judges and makes war (Revelation 19:11) named Christ Jesus, for whosoever will that wants to be saved in these last days. I don't own heaven or hell to put you or me in, but through the hand of the Lord on my life, I have been given the keys and granted access to the knowledge of the Kingdom of God here on earth. This is so that I can complete the good work assigned to me before the foundations of the world. With assurance through my documented experiences, numerous witnesses to my life change, and written testimony, I can say that I am now inching closer to who God intended me to be. I was born to a woman of God who wasn't even supposed to have children, yet she had two. I lived a life that should have ended in death and hell too many times without count, yet I am here not by the luck of this world or my own accord but by His Grace, Mercy, Love, and His Peace for the intended purpose He has for my life. So please be enlightened and blessed by this book written for inspiration, instruction, and knowledge through the Holy Spirit for a time such as this.

ROOT OF FALSE TEACHING ...FALSE VISION AND DIVINATIONS

Then the LORD said to me, "The prophets are prophesying lies in my name. I have not sent them or appointed them or spoken to them. They are prophesying to you false visions, divinations, idolatries, and the delusions of their own minds (Jeremiah 14:14 NLT).

The First Expose: False Teaching and Visions

False teachings and false visions are major stumbling blocks to afflicted individuals. The term "afflicted individuals" depict all humanity throughout this book because the Bible says we all suffer from our sinful nature (Romans 3:10). The word "afflicted" means one affected by a disease that causes or tends to cause bodily pain or mental distress. For some, throughout history, the consequences of not obeying The Word of God were the primary source of affliction then and still is today. Need proof? All of us have a mandatory date with a box. The only people not in some form of distress or anxiety over the matter, whether it be ignorance or denial of this fact, are the ones who are already dead! Rest for your souls is only attained through Christ Jesus, who God and a great set of witnesses before and after Him testified of this truth. We will discuss much more of that topic later. Nothing

27

is hidden from God, whether our blatant outward transgressions against others or our secret inward thoughts and attitudes. The problem for most in this generation is that they do not believe they are afflicted. Most think or feel they are not afflicted because we live in ignorance, denial, and delusions apart from our Lord and Savior, Christ Jesus. Rejection of the actual costs of being a disciple of Christ Jesus steadily increases living in this upside-down world and will always be a breeding ground for false teachings. While seeking the will of God for our lives, some struggle to receive a consistent, sound doctrine from our teachers and even in personal study time by misreading and misinterpreting scriptures. False teachings and visions are a product of people who may or may not have heard from God but have a compromised message for His current will for His people in this season invalidated because their prophecies go unfulfilled (Deuteronomy 18:22). Many pastors, preachers, and teachers continue to say, "God said," and when it doesn't happen, they move on to the following lying vision with no remorse or fear of God. As bad or worse, some Christians show undying loyalty to these individuals who are not accountable to anyone.

God's will for His people in the beginning and still today is that we are a nation in Christ Jesus, Holy unto Himself.

However, the false prophet or teacher's intent is possibly confused with relaying their own will of what they want God to do, in lieu and regardless of the immediate plans and purposes God is preparing His people for in this particular season. For example, if a pastor, teacher, or preacher is impartial or hypocritical, practices and condones hating their brother made in the image of God, how is that person expected to hear a word from the Lord? The foundation of God's Kingdom is mercy and righteousness (Psalms 89:14), and He desires truth in our inward parts. Only the called who are pure in heart should seek God to impart in us true wisdom to speak on His behalf (Psalms 51:6). The Holy Scriptures say that we should not all strive to be teachers because teachers are judged more strictly (James 3:1). To the false prophets of old, God said He would send strong delusions so that they would believe a lie, therefore producing inaccurate manifestations of current unfolding events which they have falsely predicted (2 Thessalonians 2:11-12). These false predictions have brought about significant concerns for Bible-toting, judgmental, condemning, and for the most part, unloving people detached from the heart of God.

Three facets of God's people who give false visions and prophecies fail to acknowledge are His CPE (compassionate,

passionate, and empathetic) nature which is the heart of God and found in one place, our Lord, and Savior Christ Jesus.

1.) God is compassionate about His people and creation (Exodus 34:6). There is no misunderstanding from Genesis to Revelation about the length God will go to deliver his people from bondage and harm to achieve his purposes for their lives (2 Timothy 2:19).

2.) God is passionate about His Word (Isaiah 55:11). The Bible says God watches His word to perform it (Jeremiah 1:12), and another place the Bible says God is not a man that He should lie or the son of man that He should repent. Will I say it and not do it? (Numbers 23:19). God's relentless passion makes Him the sovereign and all-powerful being that defines His immortal, unchanging demeanor, and character.

3). Finally, the empathetic nature of the CPE of God is vehemently displayed in and through Christ Jesus, the Lamb of God sacrificed for all humanity. God's love, faithfulness, grace, and mercy for His children, including purposefully giving up His One and Only Son, Christ Jesus, to die in place of you and me (John 3:16). The biggest flaw with the false prophets today is that they never exhibit any accountability, humility, or love for all people necessary to be a spokesperson here on earth for the Only True Most High God in heaven. The partiality and hypocrisy they exhibit that divide, oppress, and persecute are not reflective of the God in Christ Jesus, who came and died so that anyone who believes in His name might be saved. This same line of thinking is what God said about His prophets or spokespersons in Jeremiah. Those prophets, as are the prophets today, are rooted in a grave error, misunderstanding, or subsequent denial of who God is, who they are, and what the end game looks like for God's plan for this world and every person that has and will ever live in it. The Bible explains that we are made in the image and likeness of our Creator. Image means character and likeness referring to our functionality or behaviors. Yet, it is also clearly stated that God is not a man but a Living, Sovereign, and Divine Spirit who is the Creator of the universe and everything in it. In these first five chapters, we will discuss some attitudes, thoughts, and behaviors that disconnect us from the will of God in Christ Jesus in these last days. The cares of this world, our understanding or lack thereof, thousands of years of strategic deception by the enemy, our self-inflicted predisposition, and our flawed state of being have compromised the clarity of some Christians. The book starts with the perspective of the first key Jesus said we all must seek. Obedience in this area results in all things added unto us. This first key begets authority, which gives knowledge, wisdom, and understanding that connect and guide us to other keys we may have missed before in the Word of God. This book identifies certain words and phrases as the flip side. Understanding the flip side is critical to understanding the spiritual realm. A large portion of the Bible is written in parable form so that only those who genuinely seek the Lord can find Him. The Bible frequently has hidden words and meanings that require the assistance of the Holy Spirit to decipher. To get proper context, something is usually a prerequisite or consequence, and you need to research and find out what it entails to ensure you get the point. Christ Jesus said the words I speak are Spirit and life (John 6:6). For many, if you are not "Spiritually" intuitive, you will strive to no avail to understand spiritual and eternal realities and truth in a time-oriented, natural, and sensual way. The Bible says the eunuch, while trying to read the Book of Isaiah, was approached by the Apostle Philip, who asked him if he understood what he was reading. The eunuch replied, "How can I know unless one guides me?" (Acts 8:31). One of the mysteries of the Bible that we are still finding out is that God has designed all things for a specific time of manifestation.

The Bible is still unfolding right before our eyes, and using our natural senses in a spiritual world will leave us depleted and exhausted because it won't work! Chapter Two outlines why people can't figure out the holiness of God because they have no idea who they are! Really! I am not talking about walking around with low self-esteem or self-worth; I'm talking about having the humility required to see who you are in the grand scheme of things and Who and where God is! Chapter Three connects who we are and what is necessary to be a disciple of Christ Jesus. We must understand the enormous price paid for our sins and the requirement mandated to all of us who voluntarily choose to live eternity with Him who will be the King of the earth. The fourth chapter identifies a pattern among the children of God throughout history to this very day. The rejection of God, His One and only Son, and now the Holy Spirit's will for our lives has left us out of options for this generation. It's either Jesus or bust, and you must choose quickly. Chapter Five highlights the problems incurred by believers of all nations that have latched on to one aspect of Jesus over the entirety of who He is, why He came, what He is doing now, and what He is coming back on the last day to accomplish.

Chapter One

THE FLIP SIDE

"For my thoughts are not your thoughts, neither are your ways my ways, saith the LORD. For as the heavens are higher than the earth, so are my ways higher than your ways, and my thoughts than your thoughts," (Isaiah 55:8, KJV). "See, I have set before you today life and good, death, and evil," (Deuteronomy 30:15 KJV). "A way seems right to a man, but its end is the way of death," (Proverbs 14:12 NKJV). But He turned and said to Peter, "Get behind Me, Satan! You are an offense to Me, for you are not mindful of the things of God, but the things of men," (Matthew 16:23 NKJV).

The First Expose: The Flip Side

What is the flip side? The Flip Side Principle of the Kingdom of God is a principle and term used in this work to describe, correlate, and connect the difference between the natural, visible, and temporary things of this world compared and opposed to the spiritual, invisible, and eternal things of the Kingdom of God on earth and heaven. The flip side principle speaks to the reasoning of God, the Maker and Creator of all things. God, in His extraordinary wisdom, made everything in the beginning "good" (Genesis 1:4-31). On the other hand, in his ongoing rebellion and disobedience, humanity has sought to "recreate," unravel, rename, and redefine everything God, in His superior wisdom, has completed (Genesis 2:2).

The Flip Side Principle of the Kingdom of God states that for whatever a thing is, there is a polar opposite thing of which it is not. A man is not a woman, and a woman is not a man. Good is not evil, and evil is not good. Why red is red, blue is blue, and green is green is as simple as because God said it is! The Lord created everything seen and unseen to be used and operated according to His divine and eternal blueprint. This world, its unbelieving scientists and philosophers, do not readily acknowledge the spiritual realm describing it as a hoax, conspiracy theories, and mere human religion. Though the skeptics admittedly understand very little by the multitude of creation theories and, to date, have never created anything that was not here already, they remain obstinate and defiant. Many still live in denial despite God's track record and the consistency of the scriptures regarding His plans, purposes, and divine will for this earth and our lives. The Bible purposefully says that a spiritually undiscerned man's wisdom cannot attain spiritual knowledge, but a person filled with the Holy Spirit compares spiritual things with spiritual. "The natural man cannot receive the things of the Spirit of God, for they make no sense to him because they are spiritually discerned. The spiritual man judges all things because he has received the mind of Christ," (I Corinthians 2:13-16).

A Kingdom-focused preacher and pastor I follow, Dr. Tony Evans, coined a saying, "If what you see is all you see, then you have not seen all there is to be seen." This quote perfectly describes the flip side of things not readily seen. The denial or misunderstanding of the flipside principle has set the stage for three devastating mistakes humanity, and even some angels in heaven, have made throughout eternity and time.

1.) Not believing God is "exactly" Who and What He says He is, 2.) the obsession with control, power, and earthly pleasures while never fully acknowledging the will of God for our lives as His created beings, and 3.) we will always need God and cannot exist wholly or peacefully apart from Him. We are all afflicted, meaning humanity and creation have endured suffering and separation from God through our eminent mortal death. Without the finished work of Jesus Christ, we remain the object of his divine wrath (Romans 9:22).

Foolish is the only word that defines the afflicted individual who gets up every morning, breathes God's air, and gets heat, light, and energy from the sun that God in Christ Jesus made yet with no thought or reverence, all of which is bewildering to me! At night, looking in amazement at the moon and stars that He hung in the heavens, some take for granted the majesty of the God who created it and humanity. All a man beholds, seen and unseen, come from and belong to God alone. Despite the flip side principle, there is no reasoning for some, and they will always continue to deny His presence, which is very unfortunate.

The Second Expose: The Natural Man vs. The Spiritual Man

This present world testifies to the accuracy of the Holy Scriptures by its plummeting downward spiral. The spiritual man understands that we are more than this temporary outer shell of colored dirt and water (our body) that is the "EARTH suit" in which we reside. At night, looking in amazement at the moon and stars that He hung in the heavens, I consider how some could take for granted the majesty of the God who created it and humanity.

There is a predisposition in the innate nature of humanity that has made it extremely difficult and borderline impossible for individuals who are ignorant of, refuse to acknowledge, or rebel against the spiritual/invisible attributes versus the physical/visible characteristics of this world to make sense of these present times. The spiritual man understands that we are more than this temporary outer shell of colored dirt and water (our body) that is the "earth suit" in which we reside.

Every person is a servant or slave of the spirit controlling them, either God or the other spirit (evil). Every one of God is reborn of His Spirit and His word influencing our being or existence (our souls) throughout our lives in preparation for life with Him. The natural man rejects holiness and godliness to do and live life aimlessly. This seemingly highly advanced society thrives on being: 1.) technologically affluent, 2.) politically minded, 3.) consumerist-oriented, and 4.) socioeconomically indulgent, which throughout history caused more short and long-term harm than good. In the short term, from this perspective, the natural man tries to live independently of his Maker and entirely on his own, which he is incapable of doing. Humankind is a victim of self-sabotage, unleashing three enemies into the world, one of which and the most damaging resides inside himself. The long-term effects draw the natural man further away from our Maker instead of discovering His perfect will for his life. In efforts to truly see our human existence from a clear perspective and change the trajectory of the downward spiral in which we have almost hit rock bottom, we must come to terms with our predisposition, resist and subdue it. The more we know, the more prideful, greedy, uncompassionate, and reckless we have become. Fingers are always pointing outward, seldom inward, blaming, and judging others, most times hypocritically and impartially unfair about human dignity, decency, and camaraderie among people. These three predisposition states of being referred to are as 1. Man's inherent nature of comfort is opposed to truth. 2. Pleasure (lusts) above all else. 3. Self-preservation at any cost, even at the expense of one's body, spirit, and soul.

The Third Expose: Flipside Words

By mixing God's will with man's human wisdom, we often interpret some words in natural meaning that God uses in a spiritual sense or connotation. For example, good is not only what we do; good first identifies whose we are because God alone is good by His nature. Therefore, He alone determines what is good and bad and clean or unclean (Mark 10:18, Acts 10:15). Similarly, no matter how many facts you place together in each situation, in the Kingdom of God, it is not truth unless corroborated by two or more true and credible witnesses (2 Corinthians 13:1). Finally, and appropriately as this book is entitled, we will all face death in this mortal body, but that is not the end of the story! Our life choices alone, Jesus or bust, will dictate where we spend eternity! Human death is not the end because we will live forever either with God in Christ Jesus where He is or outside, apart from Him in the lake of fire and brimstone for eternity (John 5:29, Revelation 22:14-15).

God's thoughts and ways exhibit an unparalleled higher standard than our feeble, inconsistent, and selfish demeanors. Here are seven essential words associated with the Kingdoms of God and heaven used by believers and non-believers alike, having natural and flipside spiritual meanings. Truth, love, heart, holy, time, eternity, and sovereignty are words that have far-reaching eternal implications in the world to come and a subsequent spiritual character-building significance in this age.

1.) Truth in this world is optional for most, but the truth in the Kingdom is commanded and non-negotiable (Psalms 51:6). The prerequisite of truth is never about what I say, what you say, or even what they say, whoever they may be; it is only about what God said. Biblical truth is first pure, and the only pure thing in this world or universe is the Word of God. This truth is where all knowledge, wisdom, understanding are derived. Everything has its roots in the truth because the truth has been here from the beginning. Contrarily, everything that has been compromised and corrupted has got its roots and sprouted out from the original truth as well. This tactic was the enemy's plan then, and he still uses it today to pervert and distort the Word of God so that man might live in error and falsehood. For this reason, the Word of God in our Lord and Savior Christ Jesus and the power of the Holy Spirit came to the earth to give us the Truth.

The failure to discern truth puts us at the mercy of being thrown and turned to man's doctrine or our own, of which neither will ever be acceptable to God (Ephesians 4:14). Therefore, He sent us the Truth wrapped in human flesh to teach, protect, and save us from ourselves and our enemies. Today, many people profess God in Jesus Christ, but they don't honestly know Him. Jesus said the Father seeks those who worship Him in Spirit and truth (John 4:24). You must realize that you have complete autonomy over where you will end up. Once you accept the truth, no one else has power over your final destination. It is not now, nor has it ever been God's will that you should die (Ezekiel 33:11). Jesus did not get on the cross and sacrifice His sinless life in vain, but he did so obediently so that you and I may have an opportunity at everlasting life.

2.) Heart. The Bible says when you seek me, you shall find me when you seek me with your whole heart (Jeremiah 29:13). If you have any doubts, reservations, or questions about who God is and isn't and what is acceptable and unacceptable to the Lord in these last days, this is the time to straighten that out. The flip side word truth is what you must do, then this next word, the heart of man, is the why, when, and how you must do it. When the Lord says, seek me with your "whole heart," He has just in one phrases, summed up the entirety of the downfall of man from Adam unto this very day. This downfall is the inability of a man to live a life on this earth with a pure and whole heart. *Pure* meaning obeying the commandments of God, and a whole heart meaning with all our motives, intentions, and opportunities, all three. We lie to ourselves and others constantly about our true motives, but God tells us the truth about ourselves. "The heart is deceitful above all things and desperately wicked; who can know it?" (Jeremiah 17:9). Matters of the heart aren't anything new; quite the opposite, they are just profoundly ignored or referred to sensually instead of as spiritual as God relates to man's heart. Heart disease is the number one killer of the natural and spiritual man. *Offense*, which often biblically means a stumbling block or temptation to sin, is the first indicator of a person dealing with heart disease. Usually, offense occurs when people are confronted with the truth about something they don't want to change. Humanity persistently deals with heart matters, often in pretense, hypocrisy, and regret. The heart of man is divided into these areas:

Motives establish the framework of why you do the things you do. King David was a prime example of someone whose motives were upright, even though his actions were not at times. We are only human and prone to make mistakes in this EARTH suit. Having the right motive for our errors may not always alleviate the consequence, but God is gracious and faithful if we repent to forgive us. The question is, do your actions glorify you, the enemy, or God?

Opportunities speak to our temptations to choose between the commands of the Lord we profess to love and obey as opposed to our fleshly wants and desires. Often, what we say we trust and believe differs from where our faith resides based on our decisions. Many doctrines of the world today's church support knowing biblically they are not of God. When you have the chance to do good and stand for God's righteousness, do you? Or do you remain silent or complacent when confronted with and knowing the truth of God's will versus the norms of our current society? Are you the carnal Christian who rebels, disobeys, and follows their own bidding or the True Believer who denies himself and follows Christ Jesus?

Intentions: What you do does not always tell the story of why you did it. The Bible says the woman who gave a penny gave more than the person who gave out of abundance. Before you, I, and everyone who has ever lived in this world steps one foot into heaven to call it our eternal home, our hearts are searched, and our minds tested (Jeremiah 17:9-10)

43

by King Jesus to give every man his just reward. No one gets into heaven or hell by accident; it is your reward for how you have lived. Judgment will divide the entire world into two sets of individuals. Each person who has done good will attain the resurrection of life, and to those who have done evil the resurrection of condemnation (John 5:29). If your name is not written in the Book of Life, there is no expectation of any other reward besides fire and brimstone (Revelation 21:8). For good, you have been saved by faith to do the will of your heavenly Father and serve Christ Jesus. The purity of your heart in this human body, not just your belief, will decide your eternal reward (Revelation 2:19). These rewards are outlined in Matthew 5 as such:

• Blessed are the poor in spirit, for theirs is the Kingdom of Heaven.

• Blessed are those who mourn, for they shall be comforted.

• Blessed are the meek, for they shall inherit the earth.

• Blessed are those who hunger and thirst for righteousness, for they shall be filled.

• Blessed are the merciful, for they shall obtain mercy.

• Blessed are the pure in heart, for they shall see God.

• Blessed are the peacemakers, for they shall be called sons of God.

- Blessed are those who are persecuted for righteousness's sake, for theirs is the Kingdom of Heaven.

- Blessed are you when they revile and persecute you and say all kinds of evil against you falsely for My sake. Rejoice and be exceedingly glad, for great is your reward in heaven, for so they persecuted the prophets who were before you (Matthew 5:3-12).

3.) Love is an attribute that God does not exhibit only in an emotional sense as people do toward their parents, wives, kids, or significant others; love, like the truth, is the nature of God (1 John:4:16). Our love for God is first rooted in faithfulness to God alone. Jesus reiterated this concept of love rooted in obedience when He said to the people, "Why do you say you love Me, and you do not do what I say," (Luke 6:46)? Jesus also clarified that God's faithfulness to Him was not only because He was the genetically born Son but also because He was an obedient Son. Christ Jesus reiterated this concept stating, "Therefore My Father loves me because I lay down my life that I may take it again," (John 10:17). In another place, He says, "I always do what pleases the Father" (John 8:29). Love to Jesus means always doing what God says because that is His being, and we likewise obey God because we are His children. Humanity, however, finds it difficult to separate the natural love we display through our fluctuating emotions from the supernatural agape love God also requires from us. Regardless of ignorance, rebellion, or disobedience, love is the primary requirement for discipleship, and without this attribute, we cannot legitimately be a part of His Kingdom.

4.) Holy is God's term to separate who He is, what belongs to Him, and the decisive nature and distinction between Himself and all creation. There has never been anything equal to God or that can be compared to God in existence. God is Holy, and everything associated with Him is holy, and His children are required to be holy (Leviticus 20:7). Period.

5.) Time is possibly the most inconspicuous of the seven flip side words that have permanent repercussions on your future. Three attributes of time are a.) you never have enough of it, b.) you can't buy or replace it, and c.) when it runs out, you don't get a do-over.

Time is a literal place we occupy here on the earth as living beings because humans no longer live in the entity of time after their last breath in their EARTH suit. Time was created by God to provide humankind with measurements and points of reference for beginnings, ends, lengths of life, days, nights, and seasons to specify significant and repeated events. Many unwisely take time for granted until it becomes inevitably close to completion, as with sickness, old age, or the realization that the end is near.

6.) Eternity is a literal place where God lives with Christ Jesus and the Holy angels. Eternity is also the home of everything not located in time, including the Kingdoms of Satan and the dead. The scriptures say to be absent from the body is to be present with the Lord (2 Corinthians 5:8). Everyone has their beginning in eternity and will surely return there one day. The natural person does not like references to eternity because that means acknowledging a hell that all unrighteous people will someday call home. A holistic worldview of eternity is an excellent foundation for a healthy fear of God.

7.) Sovereignty is a problematic word to conceptualize for this generation whose governing body (the rich and powerful) believes in the hypocritical and partial treatment of those they deem not worthy. The manufactured terms *God-given* and *God ordained* choices concerning one's rights and privileges are often at the expense of others. Many people who consider themselves Christians have a non-biblical ideology regarding their rights versus others. The flip side of this democratic or republican style manmade government rapidly approaching its end is the Kingdom of Heaven to come ruled by Christ Jesus, King of kings and Lord of lords.

The Fourth Expose: The Flip Side: The Secret Things of God

"God is the God of order and not confusion" (1 Corinthians 14:33). "Truth, justice, righteousness, and mercy are the foundations of His Kingdom" (Psalms 89:14). God has all rights and authority to implement, exercise, and operate the flip side principle as He sees fit. Further, our Father in heaven has the right and the power to reveal, disclose, hide, accept, deny, and approve nothing, anything, or everything that He alone desires according to His pleasure and to accomplish His divine will. Period. He is God, all-knowing, all-powerful, creator of everything seen and unseen, and He does not make mistakes. Nobody but God in Christ Jesus owns heaven, earth, the universe, or a hell to put, make, create, or assign anyone or anything. Only our Lord and Savior Christ Jesus has endured and triumphed over death and the grave, earning Him alone the right to judge and rule over all creation (John 5: 23-24). In His superior wisdom, God has information He reveals plainly and some information that He hides, seals, keeps a secret, or gives in bits and pieces to humble the wise and prudent at heart. The flip side of the secret things of God is the revealed things of God (Deuteronomy 29:29). The revealed things of God for us today come from His written word found in the Holy Scriptures (Revelation 22:18-19).

48

Living in all True Believers, God's Holy Spirit agrees with our spirit, revealing Himself to us His truth of eternal life found in Christ Jesus through His blood, His word, and upon our voiced repentance. Today, we call this collection of writings or His word the Holy Bible or the Holy Scriptures. The Bible is God inspired by the Holy Spirit and contains no errors. The purpose of the Bible is salvation and sanctification for all who believe ultimately to enjoy eternal life with Jesus Christ where He is. God's most important commandment through His word is to love Him with all our hearts, minds, soul, and strength and love others as ourselves (Matthew 25:31-33). The Bible outlines in detail for Believers the requirements and the conditions desired of those He considers His adopted children (Romans 8:15). God is Holy, meaning He is set apart from anything else in all creation, in power, sovereignty, as well as where He lives in eternity because He is "eternal." Being Immortal, the First and the Last, undeniably gives Him the absolute rights and authority to have the title and position of God. As we then look at God's expectations for our lives versus our mostly fleshly and earthly expectations, hopefully, you too will agree that we serve a God who is the Master of what the Holy Spirit has shown to me as the "flip side." Though there are many reasons God chooses to keep some things hidden and a mystery, two distinct characteristics have remained unchanged throughout the history of the world: 1.)

God is forever merciful, gracious, long-suffering, good, and truthful to the just and unjust. He forgives humankind's iniquity, transgressions, and sins, but He will by no means acquit the guilty (Exodus 34:6-8). 2.) The second is also a painfully accurate depiction that the condition and disposition of humankind's inconsistent, wicked, and evil heart (Jeremiah 17:9) is an ongoing issue that God has dealt with since day one of the tragic fall of Adam and Eve in the Garden of Eden (Genesis 3:6). Therefore, God's judgment is true because He has been here from the beginning. Heaven and earth testify that there is no other like Him, and to date, His plans and purposes have never failed in the world or heaven (Isaiah 46:9-10). The Bible tells us that everything has a season and an appointed time for every purpose under the heavens. The truth that man will never figure out the hidden things of God no matter how hard or long He tries displays God's omnipotent knowledge and wisdom (Romans 11:33). No person but God in Christ Jesus has ever defeated death, controlled nature or created something from nothing. God's secret things and revealed things are given at the perfect time to regenerate and redeem the sinful man into the holy and righteous man God preordained.

• The Secret Things of God (Deuteronomy 29:29)

• The Revealed Things of God (Deuteronomy 29:29)

- The Hidden Things of God (Isaiah 48:6)

- The Sealed Things of God (Daniel 12:4) (Revelation 10:4)

- The Vision is for an Appointed Time (Habakkuk 2:3)

- The Parables of God in Christ Jesus (Matthew 13:13)

- The Mysteries of God (Colossians 2:2)

These strategies listed above used by God throughout His word are essential because wicked and evil men, like their father, Satan, have no intention of humbling themselves to God or His word. No matter the wrapping, whether modern day witchcraft, sorcery, and idolatry concealed in technology, government, and human wisdom, all will have their judgment day. Assuredly, whether revealing or concealing God's plans for us, His children, are for good and not evil. The road is often challenging, and there are many stumbling blocks, but we are comforted that God, who called us, is faithful. Doing all things in love while training ourselves in all godliness, we appreciate the flipside, understanding that it works for our good. True riches of the Kingdom are the full assurance of acknowledging and accepting the mysteries of God the Father and Christ.

Envision the Promise: 'For to be carnally minded is death, but to be spiritually minded is life and peace. Because the carnal mind is enmity against God; for it is not subject to the

51

law of God, nor indeed can be. So then, those who are in the flesh cannot please God (Romans 8:6-8).

Chapter Two

DELUSIONS OF GRANDEUR

"For if a man think himself to be something when he is nothing, he deceiveth himself. But let every man prove his own work, and then shall he have rejoicing in himself alone, and not in another," (Galatians 6:3-4). "Has not my hand made all these things, and so they came into being? Declares the LORD. "These are the ones I look on with favor: those who are humble and contrite in spirit and who tremble at my word," (Isaiah 66:2).

The First Expose: God Loves You

The Bible says, *"How often I have wanted to gather your children together, as a hen gathers her chicks under her wings, but you were not willing,"* **(Luke 13:34).** This book focuses on the "Good News" message that you will live and not die and exposes some to the riches of God found only in and through His Son Christ Jesus! However, for unbelievers, the good news for the believer is horrifying news for them. There is no question that God loves us. God demonstrated this love when He saved us while we were yet sinners (Romans 5:8). God gave up His One and Only Son as a ransom for the entire world. This work has summed up the many reasons God sent His Son into the world to give us knowledge of these four truths:

- Who God is (John 14:9)
- Who Jesus Christ is (John 1:34)
- Who we are with and without Him (Philippians 4:13, John 15:5)
- Who the Holy Spirit is (John 14:26).

This world and Satan, the enemies, have made it extremely difficult for people to find God because of twisting and denying the truth. This generation's professed highly technological individuals daily find ways to discredit the hand of God. Many politically motivated individuals use the government and religion to oppress the poor and control the streams of wealth. The average consumerist and socioeconomically minded people need minimal swaying to indulge in immorality. The enemy has successfully deceived many into believing God's ways are now somehow obsolete. Seeing our human existence for what it truly is means acknowledging the downward spiral in which we are almost at the bottom. Humanity's downward spiral is rooted in the lusts of the eyes, the lusts of the flesh, and the pride of life (1 John 2:16). As it was in the beginning, when Eve, deceived by the devil, sought wisdom like God illegitimately, instead of the loving wisdom from God that makes one truly wise, it set off a traumatic chain of events, relinquishing power, dominion, and rulership to the enemy. These events, the likes of which we still have not yet fully recovered, won't be wholly corrected until the Day of Jesus Christ (Revelation 21:6). It seems the more people know, the more prideful, greedy, less compassionate, and reckless they have become. Sounds familiar? Yes, this happened in the days of Noah when the Bible says the evil in man's heart had gotten out of control, so much so that God repented that He ever made man and concluded to wipe them off the face of the earth, except for Noah and his family of seven who found grace (Genesis 6:8). Fast forward to now in the 21st century, as we rapidly approach the second installment the Good Lord promised, and we coin "the Days of Noah Part II: The Reign of Fire," we are on the verge of maxing out once again. The closer we approach the fulfillment of the Gentiles (Romans 11:25) (they are the remnant chosen by God covered during this season of grace), the worst this society will become. Despite many years of being warned, the people of Noah's day refused to repent of their ungodly ways. We, professed Christians having a fully completed Bible and a great set of witnesses, what on earth kind of excuse will we have when the judgment of the Day of Christ comes? No, the truth is we are pretty messed up today, generally denying anything that looks like God or the will of God for this world that He alone created.

I can remember as a youth attending the "holiness Church" of my grandmother in my father's family a few times. The hours spent in their all-day church services felt like an overreach. I needed to understand why all the shouting, passing out, and unknown languages spoken were necessary. I wondered why the people at my Methodist church did not conduct their services or themselves the same way. Looking back, I know Grandma's generation had it right, and these future generations would initiate the decline of what this work identifies as the True Church and the True Believers. The True Church is the church that Christ Jesus built and the only church He is returning for that will not receive judgment (Matthew 16:18). The True Church consists of True Believers. These are the followers and disciples of Christ Jesus who have been:

- Reborn of water and Spirit (John 3:3)

- Not of the will of man (John 1:13)

- Not of the will of the flesh (John 1:13)

- Not of blood (John 1:13)

- Confess with their mouth and believe in their heart (Romans 10: 9-10)

- Testimony of Christ Jesus and keep the commandments of God (Revelation 11:17)

- Have the seal of God (2 Corinthians 1:22).

The previous two or three generations have failed to prioritize God's Kingdom. One reason is that they have no idea what God's Kingdom is or its purpose. Just about every activity of the church has been labeled "Kingdom" in our present times. In contrast, this generation has utterly ignored and forgotten what it means to be separate, holy, salt, and a light to the world. We have confused treating others with basic human dignity, decency, and camaraderie for an opportunity to infuse and partake in this world's ungodly activities. When Jesus commanded His church to go into all the world, teaching all nations, tribes, and tongues among all people, the purpose was to deliver the Good News; the law no longer condemned us (Romans 8:1). The "Good News" was not just for certain races, genders, and people of a specific socioeconomic status; it was a choice everyone would have the opportunity to make. There was only one condition, peace resided with those who accepted Jesus and His word, but those who rejected the Word were on their own (Luke 10:10-12).

The Second Expose: Reconditioned

Humanity has suffered three types of reconditioning, affecting a man's heart that changed the perfect man God made in His likeness and image into someone unacceptable to his Creator. This new character and behavior manifested themselves into these three subdivisions that dominate the heart of man in this current age:

• Man's inherent nature of comfort is opposed to the truth

• Pleasure (lusts) above all else, in opposition to the law of God

• Self-preservation and control at any cost, in opposition to the righteousness God demands of this world and everyone.

This need for control comes even at the expense of one's very own body, spirit, and soul, if necessary, to save the outer image regardless of how detrimental it is for us and others. Some people don't presently have the capability or capacity to understand spiritual things yet consider themselves intelligent and practical. Most people don't want to know the truth about what's wrong with them and will continue to play Russian roulette with their eternity until their date with their box, which is an appointment no man will miss or until the first PLANE (the rapture) comes and goes, which we will discuss in a later chapter.

After the fall of man, the effects of our new predispositions automatically reject anything that involves suffering, loss of control, or the absence of some instant, perceived, or delayed form of gratification. The flesh doesn't like truth because truth offends our control center when it is not in the interest of one's motives.

These present times continue to unveil the hearts of men filled with abominable and detestable exploits providing evidence that we live in perilous times, unlike anything we have experienced before, but by no means is it anywhere near where it is destined to one day come fulfillment. Few life lessons in this E³ART³H suit are more disheartening and demoralizing to the human ego than coming to terms with who we are not versus who we deceitfully tell ourselves and others we are. This phenomenon isn't new. Humanity and the angels alike have suffered from what this work calls "delusions of grandeur," which contributed to the original fall of man. Humankind's motivations, intentions, and opportunities have been skewed to reflect the enemy and mimic his nature. The consequence of rebellion and disobedience introduced sin and death upon humanity. This writing encourages basic Holy Scripture precepts and principles to help people deal with their heart issues. We are not talking about cults, strange teachings, my version of what

I thought it meant, what I heard anybody say, or anything else. This book relays what The Spirit says to the "True Church" in a season and a day such as the current one we are experiencing. The Bible says, "Do not be deceived for God is not mocked, for whatever a man sows, he will also reap (Colossians 2:8).

The Third Expose: Jesus Loves You!

There is no doubt that our Lord and Savior, Jesus the Christ, loves us, who though innocent and blameless, was crucified and murdered for no other reason than to save a world that was dead in their sins. So, to rephrase the million-dollar question of "does God in Christ Jesus love you?" Yes, He inexplicably does. Unfortunately, humankind tends to concentrate on the sensual and temporary parts. At the same time, Jesus is concerned with your complete framework, namely the holistic and eternal aspects of your spirit and soul. The Bible tells us that your soul and spirit will return to God for judgment of everything it has done in the body. "Don't take my word for it," Jesus said. "Do not worry then about those who can only kill the body, but fear God who can destroy the body and the soul in hell" (Matthew 10:28).

My assignment and goal in my time left in this EARTH suit are to expose whosoever wills to the truth and offer them the opportunity to choose life, eternity with God rather than death, eternal separation from God. The Bible says, "Go into all the world, make disciples of all nations, baptizing them in the name of the Father, and of the Son, and the Holy Spirit, and teaching them to obey everything I have commanded you" (Matthew 28:18-20). My efforts are to write the vision and make it plain that people who live like I once did can experience life and salvation. "If you love them like you say you do, write the books." This is what I was told to do, and this is how I am fulfilling my Kingdom assignment. All believers can agree that the time is nearer now for believers and unbelievers alike than at any other time in history for the return of our Lord and Savior to retrieve his church.

The Fourth Expose: Do You Love Yourself?

The real question people do not ask is, do you love yourself, or do you only consider the parts of you that are dying daily? Most people, at face value, don't even understand what that means. I'm talking about your body, spirit, and soul. Not just the part that you see in the mirror every day, but also the attributes that feel, think, love, hate, get angry, get happy, get sad, feel pain and disgust, the nature in you that when you want to do right, you still end up doing the opposite of what you know to do. Do you love that part of you? Automatically most, of course, say you do, discounting those who suffer from low self-esteem and other emotional and psychological issues.

Nevertheless, most do not realize that your words don't match your actions, lifestyle, or worldview. Those not-so obvious parts of you are the main parts God is gravely concerned about in the complete you. The Bible says, as far as your outer shell, the mortal part of you, called your body, is concerned from the dust you were created and to the dust you shall return (Genesis 3:19). The flesh profits nothing, nor can it inherit the Kingdom of God (1 Corinthians 15:50). Though your human body undergoes decay, your spirit and soul will return to God. People don't know who they are; most in this generation want to be left alone. Very few are interested in their spirit after mortal death, which is a huge mistake. Naturally, God being God, this disconnect resulted in separation from the presence, blessings, and daily communing with their heavenly Father. This false sense of security creates complacency and arrogance despite the Holy Scriptures stating that we should not think more highly of ourselves. We should use sober judgment and the intelligent perspective of our importance retrospectively to the grace and mercy God has shown us in Christ Jesus. The failure to make daily attempts toward a healthy and honest relationship, first with the Lord and second with ourselves, has had two deceptive and devastating effects on our short lives. First, we continue the same paths that led us to the initial separation remedied through our Lord and Savior, Christ Jesus. Second, our pride and denial of our estranged relationship with our Creator have blinded us to the limitations of these E³ART³H suits and the remodeled lives we experience in them.

The Fifth Expose: E³ART³H Suit

Every person in the world is in an E³ART³H suit. When birthed into this world, the chemical makeup of every living being is approximately seventy-five percent water, and the rest of the body is the exact biological makeup of the dirt in a well-cultivated backyard. While we are spending all our time killing, oppressing, and persecuting each other, no one wants to acknowledge or come to some form of realization we all are a different shade of dirt. That's it. There is nothing more particular about the white man, the black man, and the Native American except the color of the soil you wear. Your outer shell or body is, in essence, your E³ART³H suit. E³ART³H suit is an acronym for "Expendable, Expiring, Excommunicated, Artificial, Remodeled, Temporary, Time sensitive, and Terminally ill House." Only the Word of God goes into extensive detail, with witnesses of the creation, modification, and demise of every living person that has lived on this earth. Despite all that humanity does to downplay the hand of God, all roads of creation lead back to God. Here is the meaning of the E³ART³H suit.

Expendable. Three things make you expendable: 1.) Does your name divide time as in AD or BC? 2.) Do you have or own heaven or hell that you can place anyone in, or pull somebody out, including yourself? And finally, 3.) Do you or do you not have a mandatory and unbreakable date with a box in which you won't be late and is approaching sooner than later? If any of these circumstances do not apply to you, feel free to close this book immediately! But it could be in your best interest, long and short term, for everybody else to hear me out. The Bible says, "But in the day that you eat of the tree of the knowledge of good and evil, you will surely die," (Genesis 2:17). Anything that perishes can be considered expendable. The Bible says, by the sweat of your brow, you will have food to eat until you return to the ground from which you were made. For you were made from dust, and to dust you will return (Genesis 3:19). These facts are hard but accurate and appropriate, making your E³ART³H suit expendable.

Expiring: You came prepackaged with an expiration date attached to you. Let's be clear on some things that may be a little confusing. First, no matter how well you take care of your body, you can't extend your life one day past the date you are supposed to leave this earth. Wisdom is taking care of yourself, which can enhance the quality of your life, but only God can extend the date of your departure. On the contrary, you can always speed up your exit from the earth through unwise living, time and chance, negligence, self-affliction, violence against you, natural catastrophes, and the like.

Excommunicated: Adam was the son of God and the first created man to occupy the earth. All sinned through one man, Adam, because we all share the likeness and image of the reconditioned man (Romans 5:12). This new predisposition has rendered all humankind excommunicated in the likeness and image of Adam and not God. Excommunication is when someone has been removed from their participation in the Christian fellowship. Sure, death is the consequence that fell upon Adam and Eve in the Garden of Eden for disobeying God (Genesis 3:19). Their disobedience further got them booted out of the garden and out of communion with God the Father in the capacity they were initially designed. The only remedy for mortal death is the rebirth by water and of Spirit, which is done through faith in the saving power of Christ Jesus alone (John 3:3).

Artificial: The E³ART³H suit you now inhabit is artificial because it is not the original, flawless, good, and perfect design God encased the original Adam. Of everything made during the first six days of creation, the only thing God considered not good was Adam's status as single because he had a suitable help mate to procreate (Genesis 2:18).

Everything God made after Adam disobeyed suffered the consequences, including the earth, animals, and nature. Humanity sustained the worst consequences, including a reconditioning of our previously blameless human bodies. This corruption simultaneously created a lifelong predisposition that has afflicted humanity to this very day. Only two documented biblical individuals have avoided the consequences of certain death in these artificial E³ART³H suits: the prophets Enoch and Elijah (Genesis 5:24, 2 Kings 211).

Remodeled: The human body has undergone a C4D5 Chronic Affliction that has rendered it susceptible to sickness, fear, and a loss of authority from the original design.
The effects of the C4D5 Chronic Afflictions are as follows:

- C4 Conditions, Compromised by the enemies

1.) The "enemy in me:" Lusts of the Eyes, Lusts of the Flesh, and The Pride of Life (1 John 2:15-17)

2.) The world, people, and materials (James 4:4)

3.) The deceiver of the whole world called

- Satan (Revelation 12:9)
- The devil (John 8:44)
- The accuser of the brethren (Revelation 12:9)

▪ Contaminated by sin (Genesis 3:6)

▪ Corrupted by disobedience and rebellion (Genesis 6:5)

▪ Condemned by unbelief (John 3:18)

D5 Dispositions:

▪ Distracted by the things and patterns of this world (Romans 12:1)

▪ Desensitized to the Holy Mandate, God in Christ Jesus requires of His children the church (1 Peter 1:16)

▪ Existing in a state of denial that humans will ever supersede the perfect will of God (Isaiah 46:11)

▪ Deceived and in danger of eternal destruction for your soul (Revelation 12:9)

▪ Delusional: given over by God to their vile passions and their debased minds, preserved for the day of wrath (Romans 1:28)

T1 Temporary: The Bible says, "You don't even know what will happen tomorrow! Your life is but a vapor; it appears for a little time then vanishes away," (James 4:14). Why would anyone who claims to be intelligent choose to play Russian roulette with their eternity? Do they not know that they have a spirit and a soul that will live somewhere after the imminent demise of the body, and only their choices here and now will control where they will spend eternity?

T2Time Sensitive. An accurate and true saying is a man is of a few days and full of trouble (Job 14:1). The only known place that your existing body can operate and function in the universe as we know it, without any artificial assistance or means (spacesuit, shuttle, ship, etc.) is in the confounds of this reality and this atmosphere called earth. It would be of great benefit for you to know the scope and limitations of this body you have for one eternal consequential reason; your spirit and soul will live and not die forced hand.

T3 Terminally Ill. The Word of God says my people die because of lack of knowledge. Rejecting truth about life and judgment does alleviate the problem or dysfunction. It only delays the inevitable. The complete personal being can't be stressed enough. We are a body, soul, and spirit, not one but three parts. You have learned that you are much more than your outer shell that is daily perishing. You have a date with a box, the only date you will not miss in your life, and you won't be late. There is no getting around it. But glory is to God in Christ Jesus that while we were yet sinners, God gave us a way of escape through His Son on the cross.

You only get one chance to live this life. The mortal house you inhabit has an eternal spirit and soul that will live forever somewhere. The beautiful promise of our Lord and Savior, Christ Jesus, in one of His final pleas to humanity is "whosoever will, may come." This open invitation is to anyone who receives the good news of eternal life and chooses Jesus the Christ as their Lord and Savior and will someday live with Him forever.

House. The human body has the likeness of our Creator. His eternal makeup is the Father, The Son, and The Holy Spirit, all three making Him one complete being. We have a body that contains or houses a spirit and a soul, making us a whole living being. This earthly house, however, is not our eternal home. At an unknown time, we will shed this earthly house for an eternal home with Christ Jesus, which we will discuss in detail in the Kingdom Alignment Principle for Implementation & Transformation (KAP IT) precept NICHE.

The Fifth Expose: Delusions D5

People who don't know who God is can't fully appreciate Christ Jesus and the finished work of the cross because they don't know who they are. It is incredible to me to watch proud people. There is a straightforward reason why they do not understand the spiritual things of this world despite living in a two-third spiritual EARTH suit themselves. The conflict unbelievers have with their natural hard heart ruling over the heart of flesh Jesus is trying to give them has caused them to live in a delusion. The gift of everlasting life for my sinful life to those who believe is a deal too good to pass up, but to those with popularity or access to large sums of money secondary if that. This dilemma is what Jesus talks about when he says how hard it is for the rich to inherit the Kingdom of God (Matthew 19:23-24). Now that you have a clearer understanding of the Kingdom of God here on earth, you see why it is a conflict of interest for rich people to understand the concept that you can't worship God and money (Matthew 6:24). People are in denial of their sole purpose, which is to serve God in Christ Jesus (John 13:20). We are encouraged to live our lives wisely, making the most of our time but understanding the Lord's will is in these evil last days (Ephesians 5:15-17). God has no equal and no rival, and anyone who challenges his divine wisdom and knowledge in no better way to explain it is a fool. Only a person with a delusional and pride-filled heart could conclude that they could overturn the will of God. Those of us who know God and seek His face daily comprehend fully why the sacrifices of God are a broken spirit and a broken and contrite heart. The Bible says these God will not despise (Psalms 51:17). The only thing we honestly give God that He doesn't already own is our praise and our thanks for first being God, good, and loving us so much that he died so that we might live. Delusion of grandeur is why people deny their sole purpose: to serve God in Christ Jesus and serve others to seek a life filled with temporary, fleeting fame, wealth, and riches. A proper and healthy understanding of who you are in your EARTH suit best manifests when you sincerely understand who you are not. When you realize that you don't deserve most if not all the things you want, then and only then can you really and fully understand the grace, mercy, and love given toward us through and in Christ Jesus unto God and by the power of his Holy Spirit.

Envision the Promise. "The Lord is your keeper, the Lord is your shade on your right hand," (Psalms 121:5).

Chapter Three

A PIECE OF JESUS

"If anyone comes to Me and does not hate his father and mother, wife and children, brothers and sisters, yes, and his own life also, he cannot be My disciple. And whoever does not bear his cross and come after Me cannot be My disciple," (Luke 14:26-27). "He who finds his life will lose it, and he who loses his life for My sake will find it. He who loves father or mother more than Me is not worthy of Me. And he who loves son or daughter more than Me is not worthy of Me," (Matthew 10:37-39).

The First Expose: All or Nothing

There is only one Way to the Father, and He is the two in one Son of God and the Son of Man, Jesus Christ (Acts 24:14). A grave error has occurred in interpreting the Holy Scriptures that is evident in the lack of fear of God in this world. The foolish heart and mind (Romans 1:21) of humanity, mixed with the denial of the will of God, combined with an inaccurate worldview of who we are as created beings, have led to a "Piece of Jesus" mentality for many Christians living in these last days. First things first, let us understand the misused word *Christia*n. The term *Christian* was first used at the first-century church located at Antioch (Acts 11:26). *Christian* was the title given to disciples who were taught by the prophets and accepted the gospel's message. However, being a disciple is no longer the criteria for being a faithful Christian during this age. The term *disciple* is rarely associated with or used by professed Christians of this era because anyone can claim to be a Christian without any proof. People who practice lying, cheating, persecuting, fornicating, and oppressing with no repentance, no turning to God, and no works befitting repentance (Acts 26:20) still profess themselves as Christians. It's almost like they live a once-a-Christian, always a Christian mentality, be it far from the truth.

On the other hand, *discipleship* sounds too much like *discipline*, and only a few Christians are interested in the instruction and self-control discipleship demands. Individuals who operate in a piece of Jesus' mentality are professed Christians who exchange the truth of the holy mandate of God's children to deny oneself, stop sinning, worshiping earthly treasures, worldly desires, passions, and riches. These individuals insist on holding onto things of the world yet simultaneously maintain their salvation and eternal rewards in the afterlife. Even though the Bible tells us in multiple places that we must choose, they follow the doctrines of men that fulfill the desires they crave. Holy Scriptures like "you can't serve God and mammon, you can't drink of the Lord's cup and cup of demons, and you cannot partake of the Lord's plate, and demons too lose in an uncovenanted and delusional religious sham (1 Corinthians 10:21).

The "Piece of Jesus" mentality is prevalent in this age primarily due to a limited understanding of the hand of God and some due to the hardness of people's hearts. Jesus had many disciples at the beginning of His ministry, but as He revealed more and more of the truth to them, they began to fall off. They were down for the fish sandwich, were in line for the healing, and were excited for the promise of eternal life but were not receptive to the costs involved. Christ Jesus made it clear either you are with me or against me, either you are a gatherer or a scatterer (Matthew 12:30). The bottom line reiterated throughout this work is you will live and not die, and every man must decide on one of two choices regarding his eternity for which he alone is responsible. Jesus said, either you are my sheep or a goat. The sheep symbolizes God's beloved children, the people of the promise, the individuals destined to remain with Him forever in eternity. The other side of the coin is the goats who refuse to know God, believe God, and turn from their wicked ways.

Some pastors, priests, teachers, and evangelists negate the flip side of the Good News as if it has no bearing on the final destination of your soul. These individuals would like to keep

Jesus inside this pretty little box filled with unconditional grace, mercy, love, and peace for all humanity. The problem is that's not what Jesus said He came to do or even who He was as the Savior of the entire world. Only a person suffering from a severe case of the Piece of Jesus mentality could confuse so many straightforward Bible verses. Holy Scripture references such as: "I did not come to make peace but a sword" (Matthew 10:34), "I did not come to abolish the law and the Prophets," (Matthew 5:17), or "if you do not repent, you will perish too," (Luke 13:3). Some deceived Christians who disregard the Word, and the holy things of God have no clue that the Jesus some people worship every Sunday in the church building is not the same Jesus of Abraham, Isaac, Jacob, and the True Church the Bible teaches. The spiritually incarcerated are believers habitually attracted to false teaching, false visions, and false doctrines given by false prophets. These false prophets aim to mislead and uplift spirits by providing illegitimate hope to the hopeless for influence or monetary or social gain. There is a significant difference between joy found in a covenant relationship with one True God and happiness associated with how you feel about the circumstances and situations in this fleeting world.

Happiness is a temporary emotion related to what is going on around you, with you, or even to you. Happiness is predicated on how a person presently feels and thinks. The same thing that makes you extremely happy today can make you sorrowful tomorrow. Joy has little or nothing to do with what's happening outside of your body but is bolstered by what's happening inside you. Joy might not make you feel good presently, but it is rooted in the complete picture and the final result coming to fruition. It did not make Jesus happy to go to the cross, but for the joy set before Him, He endured it to the death, understanding not His will but the Fathers (Luke 22:42-44). The joy of the Lord is a result of a supernatural and satisfying internal contentment with eternal consequences. This concept relays a different perspective from the joy of this current generation, whose primary objective is instant gratification, pleasure, and convenience. The joy of the Lord found in Christ Jesus through the power of the Holy Spirit, which gives contentment in all things, eventually produces true happiness. There is no comparison between God's righteous unchanging, faithful love and the world's fluctuating, emotionally induced sensual love that manipulates and deceives them. We don't deserve anything we have; it is a gift manifested by the grace of God.

If not identified and corrected, a stumbling block many will have when they get to heaven's gate is their Peter experience. In one of Peter's last conversations with the Lord, he wanted to know the plans for the other disciple, John, after learning details about his future and how he would die. Jesus rebuked him and said, "Don't worry about him, you follow me," (John 21:22). Many today expect comparison to what they deem "the bad people," thinking they will be justified compared to others, especially the world. There are three significant problems with this theory. First, the world is already condemned because of unbelief (John 3:18), so they don't count. Second, Jesus, the Word of God alone, is the goal and standard. The scriptures say we are predestined to be conformed to the image of the Son, Christ Jesus, the first of many brethren to come (Romans 8:29). Third, the Holy Spirit has come into the world to convict the world of sin, righteousness, and judgment while leading and guiding believers into all truth (John 16:9,13). You are responsible for yourself, no one else.

The Second Expose: The Lord

The first requirement to avoid the piece of Jesus mentality is the confession with one's mouth that Jesus is your Lord. *Lord* means your worship, service, and life belongs to Jesus, who alone saved you. You are no longer your own because you belong to the Lord (1 Corinthians 6:19-20). For a familiar reason, this precept significantly downplays a critical aspect of the salvation process. The nature of humanity seeks control over every part of its lives. Giving up control of one's life and giving it to the Lord is a process called sanctification and is only possible with the assistance of the Holy Spirit. Relinquishing control of one's life is impossible for a natural person to grasp. Unless you clearly understand who God is, discussed in the Flip side, and accept who you are discussed in Chapter Two, Delusions of Grandeur, you will undoubtedly be serving and living with an unacceptable "Piece of Jesus" mentality.

In April of 2021, the Holy Spirit posed two questions to ask my 16-year-old son, who, as he grows older, becomes more and more fascinated with temporary stuff and material wealth, despite all the blessings he has seen firsthand from the Lord. The first question was, "what does that do," and the second was, "where are you going to go with that?" The questions stemmed from this Bible scripture: "For what profit is it to a man if he gains the whole world and loses his soul, or what can he give in exchange for his soul," (Mark 8:36-37)? Indeed, if you are going to live and not die, everything you have and do on this earth that does not serve Jesus Christ is futile. In our vain attempts to capture material, temporary, and perishing things of this world, what does it do for us in the end? If there is nothing after this life, then we have still lived in vain if we lived it not to help others. Some, like me, know for sure and far more simply believe by faith there is a realm called eternity to look forward to after this life.

The Third Expose: The Savior.

The second aspect of your salvation is the belief that Jesus was raised from the dead in your heart (Romans 8:34). Our motives, intentions, and opportunities reflect our faith and trust with the heart. Accepting Jesus as your Savior is just as important as trusting Jesus to be your Lord. People's actions suggest they have no problem with Jesus the Savior. However, this confused generation still prefers navigating their own lives, even after realizing the little control they have. The problem is accepting Jesus Christ as your Savior means you have a reasonable responsibility to serve Him with your body (Romans 12:1). This worldview is a problem for a generation that believes the Bible authorizes them to do whatever they want. Abortion, fornication, adultery, idolatry, and falsely relying on the grace of God without true repentance will cover it. Why? "God knows my heart" is the answer and reason many give today to justify sinful behavior and rebellion. Yes, He does know your heart, and this confession is of no help to you but, in all likelihood, a witness against you if not confessed in true repentance.

This belief poses the second question, "Where are you going to go with that?" The Bible says, "Or what will a man give in exchange for his soul?" Nothing you have physically on this earth can buy your way into heaven. There was only one suitable substitute, propitiation, and ransom for my soul and yours found only in the Son of God Christ Jesus. Nothing in heaven, on earth, or under the earth was found worthy and tested except the Lamb of God to save humankind. In reality, the temporary things of this world we value and claim to be ours aren't ours. We own nothing in this life, which is one hundred percent corroborated because we take nothing from it when we die! All we can do on this earth is steward what God alone has placed here for our pleasure. None of it is of any value where you are going anyway.

The Fourth Expose: Lose This Life

As we mentioned in Chapter Two, do you really love yourself? We found out that most people are only interested in the part of them dying daily, but the other two-thirds of you, your spirit, and your soul renew daily. Because of the great price paid for the ransom of our souls, the Bible tells us that we have died to ourselves, and now we live for Christ Jesus, our Lord and Savior (Galatians 2:20). My prayer is for the unbelieving to come to some understanding of the incredible transaction that has taken place so that they might not fail an open book test and unnecessarily spend eternity in the SPA (Satan's Permanent Abode) of fire and worms that don't die. Jesus repeatedly clarifies narrow is the gate and difficult the way to eternal life. This walk of faith is not easy, and few find it (Matthew 7:14). This worldview contradicts this new age's popular teachings, professing that everyone's saved regardless of their earthly character. However, the hardest part isn't that it is unattainable in our human EARTH suit; the hard part is people's inability to deny themselves even for their eternal betterment.

The notion that we can give God a piece of ourselves when He has given us everything is preposterous and absurd. Only in a man's depraved imagination is anything like this even capable of existing. The typical man is not giving up a "ham sandwich," much less dying for someone they know and most certainly not someone they don't know and is characterized as undeserving.

Unconfirmed, but a worthy saying; nonetheless, Mahatma Gandhi is said to have quoted, "I like your Christ, but I don't like your Christians because they are so much, unlike your Christ." Regardless of where the quote originated, it is indeed valid and accurate. Though Gandhi was not a Christian, he made an observation and thought-provoking sentiment that plagues the unification of the Christian church today. One of the ways we approach Jesus in the church today is by picking out the things less confrontational to us and negating the things Jesus said that bring real change, salvation, transformation, and ultimately restoration into the life of the professed believer. We fully understand the concept that there is strength in numbers because the first thing people tend to do is assemble with like-minded individuals to encourage some validity in their actions and decisions. The thought process is if I am not the only one feeling this way or doing it this way, it must not be all wrong. Wrong answer! The Bible says, "He who walks with the wise becomes wise, but a companion of fools suffers harm. Hang out with a fool, and you become foolish (Proverbs 13:20). James concludes that a double-minded mind is like a wave on the sea being tossed and turned at every whim (James 1:8). An African proverb states that it takes a village to raise a child with the mindset that shared values and community play an integral part in the adolescent stages into adulthood. Moral consistency culminated with adult supervision is a recipe many communities, especially in low-income and poverty-stricken areas, would welcome today.

A covenantal relationship is a binding agreement between God and whosoever agrees by faith and the belief that God rewards those who trust and believe in Him. The flip side is where there is no covenant, there is no protection from God's wrath or judgment through Christ Jesus. The peace of this current generation, whose primary focus is pleasure and convenience, is contrary to the forgiving, nonjudgmental, and loving covenantal relationship that God offers His children who love Him and live for His purpose. To be a believer and follower of Christ Jesus and the Kingdom of God requires belief, faith, and the Holy Spirit, whereas the world is dependent on self-effort and the luck of the draw. The love of God in Christ Jesus is intentional and covered by the grace and mercy of God that provide confidence and security for all true Believers. The Bible says, "My grace is sufficient for thee and made perfect in your weakness," (1 Corinthians 12:9).

Therefore, the Bible says, "I told you unless the Father has sent you to me, you can't receive my teaching" (John 6:65). The question is, do you want to be changed? Most people want God to accept them as they are, and he does literally and figuratively, but there are stipulations to this process. This process is called repentance. The Lord says I will by no means acquit the guilty (Exodus 34:7). If you do not understand what it means to be holy, if you do not understand sanctification or set apart, you will have problems entering the Kingdom of God and Heaven. The hand of God is on the wicked as well as the righteous (Psalms 11:6-7). This perspective insinuates the power of God ultimately controls everything down to the last microcosm of this world; it's under his control. The Bible says, "The hand of God has the power to establish you in riches and honor while strengthening others and making great men," (1 Chronicle 29:12).

The Fifth Expose: Reborn

"Jesus answered, 'Most assuredly, I say to you, unless one is born of water and the Spirit, he cannot enter the Kingdom of God,'" (John 3:5). Again, heart disease, namely offense, has conditioned some churches today to cherry-pick the less offensive commands of Christ Jesus and altogether omit the straightforward commands that He said produce fruit or results in our walk of faith. Forsaking the pleasures of this world and even our own lives appears to be an unreasonable request for a natural person to comprehend. Real change, salvation, and restoration are only achieved in Christ Jesus. This salvation is nothing you can do on your own! At some point, your natural strength can and will fail. Only the supernatural Word of God that cleanses your heart and the blood of Jesus that clothed us in His righteousness will suffice lasting change. The "word" and "blood" are the types of water metaphorically Christ Jesus refers to when He states,

"Everyone must be reborn of water."

The hard truth is most want to keep everything the same, and some even have created a theology in which spiritual rebirth is recommended, not required. These individuals don't believe you must be reborn because of this misconception; they don't know God. Somehow, in their minds, God is Santa Claus or the Easter Bunny, and that accountability to God and our responsibility to serve Christ Jesus is optional. The Bible says, "Do not think I have come to bring peace on the earth but a sword. Nothing can come before Jesus if you choose to live as a disciple and follower of our Lord and Savior. Not your mother, brother, father, sister, wife, or kids come before Jesus. Why? You can look at it from this perspective; none of these family members have the means or ability to own heaven or hell to assign you to at the expiration of your EARTH suit. You can't honor people over the Lord and then afterward expect to live with Him in eternity. Jesus said it verbatim, "Anyone that loves father, mother, sister, brother more than me is not worthy of Me," (Matthew 10:34-39). If there ever was, this is one of those times when you can't have your cake and eat it too.

Contrary to popular belief and even teaching, this party in heaven doesn't work that way. The Bible says that some of the problems with your divided commitment are first, you will hate the one and love the other or be devoted to one and despise the other (Luke 16:13). You cannot serve mammon and God. Material things such as money, houses, cars, or socioeconomic status, none of these things that people honor and worship are more important to God than your commitment to serve Christ Jesus as Lord and Savior sincerely. One of the biggest deceptions in any afflicted individual's mindset, including my own, is the fallacy that we could ever know in our entire lives what it means, felt like, and cost Jesus on that cross. Jesus, bearing the whole weight and consequences of all humankind on his shoulders unto death, completed the offering God required of humanity is utterly astounding. Of the millions of other reasons, this one, His sinless death, is the most humbling of all, having looked back over my life and seeing how unworthy I truly am on my own.

Envision the Promise. For I am the Lord your God, who upholds your right hand, who says to you, "Do not fear for I am with you," (Isaiah 41:13)

Chapter Four
NO FOURTH OPTION

"And whosoever speaketh a word against the Son of man, it shall be forgiven him: but whosoever speaketh against the Holy Ghost, it shall not be forgiven him, neither in this world, neither in the world to come," (Matthew 12:32). He will redeem his soul from going down to the Pit, and his life shall see the light. "Behold, God works all these things, Twice, in fact, three times with a man, to bring back his soul from the pit that he may be enlightened with the light of life," (Job 33:28-30). The Bible says, "to seek the Lord while He may be found; call upon Him while He is near," (Isaiah 55:6).

The First Expose: The Will of God

It is not the will of God that any man should perish but that he should repent and live (2 Peter 3:9). There is, however, a cutoff point and fulfillment of time in which man must choose between one of two possible eternal scenarios, either; eternal life with God, acceptable in His presence, or death, being eternal separation from God, unacceptable or unworthy to be in His presence (Deuteronomy 30:15). The Bible says, "to seek the Lord while He may be found" (Isaiah 55:6). This scripture suggests that the Lord will not always show grace on our folly and told us so verbatim after dealing with the sinful man before the flood.

The word *sin* means an offense against God or all unrighteousness that does not align with the known will of God (1 John 5:17). In the book of Exodus, the Lord described His tolerance level for sin, in which He stated that He would by no means acquit the guilt (Exodus 34:7). One of the first recorded conversations between God and man about sin was the story of the first murderer Cain, the brother of Abel, called righteous. We pick up where God pleads with Cain to resist the anger, jealousy, and hostility he harbored because of his rejected sacrifice but instead do what is acceptable to God. Abel gave the first and the best of his flock, while Cain gave an offering that did not reflect the sacrifice of a pure heart but from a place of disdain, rebellion, and disobedience. Cain was mad at God for His refusal to accept His offering and then proceeded to take his anger out in violence against his flesh and blood sibling. This same disregard for the will of God and respect for his fellow man has happened even to this very day between humans of this earth, all made in the image and likeness of God, devouring each other when they can't have their way or desire for something that belongs to someone else. God still tried to warn Cain even before he committed the act physically, but in his heart, he had already deflected onto his brother, and sin entered his heart (Genesis 4:7). God's time and effort to encourage Cain to make a better decision confirms that God does His best to keep us from sinning against Him. He does this today by telling us plainly in His Word what is acceptable and unacceptable in His sight (1 Corinthians 6:9-10).

Moreover, God also is not throwing people into hell for disobeying Him. More precisely, a man chooses to go to hell because he refuses to deal truthfully with his heart and come to true repentance or a sincere turning away from things unacceptable to God. Your salvation and sanctification are not about who God is; God doesn't change. He remains faithful to His Word and promises. It's always been about who we are not. The option to choose is what the Lord said about the commandments placed before the children of Israel: choose life, not death. God is not a man that he should lie or a Son of man that He should repent (this earth and Numbers 23:19). God has been running the universe for four and a half billion earth years by man's calculation (National Geographic Society). And it's been longer than that, but that's all the scientists can come up with when they try to calculate the age of the earth, so we'll work with their math. We know, however, that God has been here from the beginning, and he will be here when it is the end. God does nothing without a cause (Ezekiel 20:44). He thoroughly outlined what "blessings" or good things associated with obedience to God are to the faithful at heart. Blessings are for our good so that we can prosper, be fruitful, and multiply as God rewards the works of our hands as he said he would in his promises. These things specifically include protection, prosperity, and long life, to name a few. On the flip side, curses are the inevitable consequences of following our corrupt minds. If you choose to disobey, the consequences of "curses" that come from disobedience inevitably affect our lives now and in the future.

The Second Expose: Man Rejected God

Here lies the problem. From the beginning, His children have been a chronic pain of consistently doing what God tells them not to do. Not only that, but they tend to get an attitude about it, too. Despite all the good God does for us daily, man's heart eventually wanders away from his perfect will for our lives for our selfish thoughts and imaginations. As Christians, this truth corroborates Holy Scripture that we seek to do our own imperfect will and not our Father's in heaven, stating none is righteous, not even one (Romans 3:10). God's Prophets, from Enoch to John the Baptist, preached and wrote under the inspiration of the Holy Spirit the Word of God, with little to moderate success and a high degree of futility due to widespread rebellion, corruption, and iniquity. This rebellion and disobedience happened within a nation that knew the will of God personally but had a long history of backsliding and spiritual blindness to the holiness of God. The Lord said to the prophet Samuel, "Listen to everything the people say to you. You are not the one they have rejected; I am the one they have rejected as their King," (1 Samuel 8:7-9). The children of Israel were guilty of turning from God and worshiping other gods, and the prophet Samuel was next in line to do what they have always done to the Lord since their exit from Egypt. Despite the warnings of mistreatment, persecution, bondage, and drafting into his military and court, they still wanted to be like the gentile nations, having a man king.

The demotion of man from dominion over fish of the sea, cattle, birds of the air, and everything that roamed on the earth occurred when man disobeyed God and sought his wisdom over God's command. Humanity brought upon himself mortal life-ending consequences because he did not believe in God. Several things transpired through this solitary act of disobedience through the first man Adam that still plagues humankind in this current world:

- He had to accept the humiliation of being evicted from his home, a place where he shared daily communion with his Father and everything he could need or want.

- He had to endure a life full of hard work, intensely working against the land that before provided for him effortlessly.

- His mate, the woman, would experience excruciating labor pains during childbirth, simultaneously bringing her joy and pain.

- He cursed himself, ultimately returning to his original state at an appointed time, for from dust he was created, and to dust, all humanity is destined to return.

The grace and mercy of God remained even after our self-inflicted judgment of the sure death of this EARTH suit, but not "eternal death of being forever void of His presence," (Genesis 6:12-24). Humankind had a glimmer of hope that would not be revealed at the time but would later be disclosed throughout the prophecy of the Bible and fulfilled in Jesus the Christ. Humanity, even the ones who know God, collectively have always made a conscious effort to test God's CPE. CPE stands for the heart of God, which is His:

- Compassion for His people (2 Chronicles 7:14)

- Passion for his Word (Isaiah 55:11)

• Empathy for His children called by His Holy name by the acknowledged sacrifice of His Only Begotten Son as a ransom for all that believe in Him (John 3:16).

Compassion for His people. God will not leave any of his children behind. He knows who His are, and He will go to any length to retrieve them because they cannot be plucked out of His hand (John 10:29). In the parable of the 99 sheep, the one missing sheep was more critical to rescue than being content with the 99 safe ones in the sheep pasture (Matthew 18:10-14). In His prayer to Father, Jesus made it a point to acknowledge that he had not lost anyone given to him besides the one written about the Son of perdition (John 17:12). Highlighted throughout the scriptures is God's passion for and in his Word. There is never any room for compromise regarding the Word of God, whether it be the written word or the Word in the flesh. There could be no mistake, and time is a witness; everything God says must and will come to pass, so much so that His spoken word even took on the form of human flesh and walked among us as the Living Word (John 1:14). The empathy of God for His children is depicted clearly in His Son Christ Jesus, who is our Witness, Savior, and the High Priest who intercedes on our behalf in heaven. God went to incredible lengths to do everything possible to save humanity, even up to and including sacrificing His Son.

God took the time and became flesh, eventually harnessing all the sin in the entire world to Himself for all humanity forever. We have stated earlier that what plagues man more than anything is his disbelief that God is Who He says He is and will do what He says He will do (Numbers 23:19). How can you flunk an open-book test? How often do you have to read, "Then you will know that I am God," to finally figure out or get a clue, God means what He says, and more than that, God is God!

There is a similarity to the baseball term and old cliche "Three strikes, and you're out" and how God uses the number three that symbolizes: harmony, God's presence, and divine completion (Numerology Center). In California and twenty-one other state courts of law, three strikes can be the difference between someone receiving probation and life in prison for the same crime depending upon the number of previous crimes that person has committed. The people of God have had two opportunities, and amid the third, as we speak, to turn from their wicked ways and serve God, in Christ Jesus and the power of the Holy Spirit that is in every True Believer.

The Third Expose: Man Rejected Jesus

Jesus clarified that His sole purpose on this first trip to the world in an EARTH suit was to give the sinful man another opportunity at salvation. The penalty for sin is death, and through Him is the only acceptable Way possible to the Father. God's plan for humanity was the propitiation, death, and righteous blood to be shed on the cross for the entire world's sins once and forever. This plan was prophesied on the flip side by the prophet Isaiah and a host of other saints that Jesus would be killed without a cause yet would not open his mouth in resistance (Isaiah 55:11). Jesus was used, misused, and repeatedly abused until the very people He came to save eventually accomplished what was in their hearts, to manipulate Him to their own will and expectations. When Jesus would not conform to their worldly expectations, He was of no more use, so they sought to kill Him. Unbeknownst to them and the enemy Satan, He had already settled in His heart and before His God to give His life freely for the lives of many (John 10:18). From the beginning of His ministry, Jesus performed miracle after miracle, and some began to believe that He was the Son of God. But He did not trust them because the Bible says Jesus knew what was in a man (John 2:24). From the beginning, Jesus saw humanity at different intervals and stages of his existence and knew what man's heart could produce. How bad was it? Jesus was perplexed about how people who were the self-proclaimed heirs of Abraham, who were supposed to know everything about His coming, were the same people who denied Him and eventually would place Him on the cross unlawfully crucified. The Bible says that a servant is not greater than His Master; therefore, if man denied God, they would deny Jesus and anyone who truly speaks God's Word to this very day.

The Bible testifies and history corroborates that sinful man rejected Jesus and His prophets. The Word of God has always warned anyone who would listen of the price of discipleship for True Believers. Our Lord and Savior, being explicit and intentional, prepared His followers for all the hatred they would incur for His name's sake. Speaking the truth so that the disciples would not be offended or surprised by the brutality of people, He stated many would be thrown out of the churches and some killed by people claiming to serve the same God the disciples love and obey. All of these things would happen because these people, in reality, didn't know God, much less the Son of God, that was sent by God Himself to save the entire world. The Bible says, "These things they will do unto you because they have not known the Father, nor Me," (John 16:3). Jesus, suffering unimaginable and horrific physical and emotional traumas, endured rejection by the very people who needed salvation the most. Jesus responded to all his critics, reminding them often of the consequences of rejecting his offer of eternal life. There is only One Way to the Father, and that Way is through the Son

Jesus the Christ (John 14:6). We are all going to take a dirt nap, and when we awaken for most or changed for those who are here at His coming, there's only one thing left to do, at the appointed time and without delay. Jesus will judge the church. This prophecy confirms what John the Baptist said He would do, even before Jesus started His earthly ministry. Most people still didn't believe them. John the Baptist acknowledged the authority, power, and ministry of Christ Jesus, saying one comes behind me who will baptize you in the Holy Spirit and fire (Matthew 3:11). The fire that John speaks of is the judgment of Christ Jesus. The Bible says to be absent from the body is to be present with the Lord. When the blood stops flowing warmly in your body and you have taken your last breath, you have transitioned from time into eternity. There is no longer any means of redemption for the earthly body once it enters the eternal state. Eternity is where our Lord and Savior Christ Jesus, the angels, and God lives. Eternity is also where the enemy Satan and his demons live. Anything that is outside of time is in eternity. Flesh and blood cannot enter eternity, but we shall also inherit our changed and glorified body, as Christ Jesus inherited in eternity. Jesus stated a profound remark about the most intricate part of salvation in this age. He takes a step back, saying that speaking against Him can be forgiven, but speaking against the Holy Spirit will not be forgiven in this age or the next. To understand what this means, we need to understand what happened with God's chosen people until this moment and move forth after His death and resurrection. After John the Baptist, from that time forth, Jesus began to teach about the Kingdom of God, a spiritual Kingdom under the guidance and teaching of the Holy Spirit (Luke 16:16). He showed His disciples through the scriptures how everything written about Him must come to pass for God's Kingdom to manifest itself. These events included going to Jerusalem and suffering many things at the hands of the elders, chief priests, and scribes. He would succumb to death, but on the third day, be raised to sit at the right hand of God (Matthew 16:21 KJV).

The Fourth Expose Man: Rejecting the Holy Spirit

"Anyone who speaks a word against the Son of Man shall be forgiven, but anyone who speaks against the Holy Spirit will not be forgiven, either in this age or the one to come," (Matthew 12:32 NLT). Powerful words of prophecy spoken here by our Lord and Savior speaking of dire and certainly severe consequences of rejecting the work of the Holy Spirit in this age and the age to come. We hear a popular sermon topic week in and week out, stating, "We are in the last days." Everybody knows it. We can see it all around us and read about it throughout the Word of God, but instead of getting better as children of God, we act like we got it all together when we know this is hardly the case in our hearts.

The Kingdom of God is entirely about the authority of the Holy Spirit living and working in the lives of the church in these last days. The significance of understanding what "no fourth option" means is rooted in the knowledge of what the Kingdom of God represents. The Kingdom of God is spiritual (Luke 17:21). In contrast, the Kingdom of Heaven is a physical presence and reign of our Lord and Savior Christ Jesus (Matthew 5:19). ***The Kingdom of God is God's accepted and man's approved spiritual will of joy, peace, and righteousness in the Holy Spirit reflected through His church on this earth that gives the power to influence whosoever wills character; (thoughts, attitudes, and behaviors) in service to Christ Jesus.*** The time of reckoning is now as far as options are concerned, starting with the church, and ending with judgment for the whole world (1 Peter 4:17). This judgment sheds insight into why blasphemy against the Holy Spirit is not forgiven in this world or the next. Rejection of the Holy Spirit is the rejection of the Kingdom of God, and whoever practices this rebellion and disobedience is destined for sheer condemnation because there is no fourth option.

The Fifth Expose: The Works

The Bible says, "Work while it is the day, for the night is coming, and no man can work." A few things come to mind when I hear this verse. 1.) We don't get another chance to relive our time spent on the earth and in this body. This season that we are currently in is the last dance before the wedding reception begins, and Jesus comes to reclaim His bride, the True Church. We need to ensure we have a few things right before we get to the wedding and be embarrassed. We are commanded to follow the straight and narrow path that leads to life versus the broad path that leads to destruction (Matthew 7:13-14). This information doesn't seem to bother some, despite a very surreal statement given by our Lord and Savior stressing, "Everyone who calls me Lord, Lord will not enter the Kingdom of Heaven." The Bible says that on that day, many will do church activities such as scripture quoting, attending church, being slain in the spirit, and all the superficial things that make individuals look like saints and Christians will not suffice. Jesus said to this select group of Christ's followers, "I never knew you; depart from me, you workers of iniquity," (Matthew 7:23). This unfortunate situation speaks to the nature of their hearts that were never really submitted fully to the gospel of Christ Jesus. The Bible says, "Don't you realize the unrighteous will not inherit the Kingdom of God?" (1 Corinthians 6:9). Don't fool yourselves. Those who indulge in sexual sin, idol worship, adultery, male prostitution, homosexuality, theft, greed, alcohol abuse, abuse, or deception—none of these will inherit the Kingdom of God (Galatians 5:21). Some of you were once like that, but you were cleansed. You were made holy; you were made right with God by calling on the name of the Lord Jesus Christ and by the Spirit of our God (1 Corinthians 6:9-11 NLT).

Understanding "No Fourth Option" gives greater insight into why blasphemy against the Holy Spirit will not be forgiven in this age or the next. As we walk out our Christian lives in this season, our progress and maturity in the faith depend on the Holy Spirit living and working in us. The Bible says, "Do not grieve the Holy Spirit that seals you unto redemption," (Ephesians 4:30). In this season, there is an epidemic level of heart disease because of lawlessness and offense; being light in a dark world is challenging. The mitigating factors, many of which we will discuss in this work, if not entirely overlooked, are characterized as conspiracy theories or over the top. These days any mention of anything that suggests some form of accountability or responsibility for building people instead of structures is avoided or discouraged at some level.

Darkness has several meanings in the Bible, referred to as a lack of knowledge, sin, and the absence of light. The lack of knowledge creates havoc and confusion when there is no Word of God to lead, guide, and direct. Darkness because of sin thrives when there is no fear of God and his judgments. Any removal of the presence of God due to rebellion and disobedience creates immediate darkness. When we try to maneuver our lives in the dark, we only stumble and subject ourselves to harm.

There will be a time when ability ceases, and judgment begins. Paul tells us that prophecy, speaking in tongues, and our human knowledge will one day vanish away (1 Corinthians 13:8-9), and the only entities that will remain of any consequence are hope, faith, and love. The New Covenant is the binding agreement that qualifies the true believer to partake in the New Age to come under the rulership of Christ Jesus. It is no coincidence that the seal that distinguishes His followers from all others is, you guessed it, love. God placed His law in our hearts and minds through the Holy Spirit, enabling us to honor and obey the Lord's commands or foolishly reject His commandments. No one will need to be overseen by another because everyone who has the Holy Spirit is ultimately accountable for themselves. The Lord is not impartial, giving us all the opportunity to experience salvation through belief in the Son, the washing with water, and the gift of the Holy Spirit (Jeremiah 31:31-34). You cannot defeat sin, death, and the grave in your limited power. Only through the authority and indwelling of the Holy Spirit living and working inside of every True Believer are you equipped to defeat the enemy. By faith with the confession of our mouth and belief in our hearts that the finished work of our Lord and Savior Jesus Christ on the cross is sufficient, we now have the power to overcome death and sin. The word of our testimony and not loving our lives to death finalizes and gives witness to how we lived our lives for Christ on earth (Revelation 12:11).

With no other options left, humanity has brought judgment upon himself. Rejecting God and His prophets, He has rejected Jesus Christ in the flesh and recently grieves the Holy Spirit with blatant disregard for the Holiness of God. Thank the Lord for new grace and mercy each day, affording us at least one more opportunity to get our houses in order! All the faithful prophets, witnesses, and saints whom the Lord has left to share His message of the Good News are waiting to reveal the sons of God and the new life promised to God's children to begin.

Envision the Promise: "Peace I leave with you, my peace I give to you; not as the world gives do I give to you. Let not your heart be troubled, neither let it be afraid," (John 14:27).

Chapter Five
TURN THE PAGE: JESUS 1.0
JESUS 2.1 THE LION

"For God so loved the world that He gave His only begotten Son, that whoever believes in Him should not perish but have everlasting life," (John 3:16). "And if anyone hears My words and does not believe, I do not judge him; for I did not come to judge the world but to save the world. He who rejects Me, and does not receive My words, has that which judges him—the word I have spoken will judge him in the last day," (John 12:47-48). "God sent not his Son into the world to condemn the world, but that the world through him might be saved," (John 3:17). "The Lord said unto my Lord, sit thou at my right hand until I make Thine enemies thy footstool," (Psalms 110:1). So when Jesus had received the sour wine, He said, "It is finished!" And bowing His head, He gave up His spirit,' (John 19:30). 'I am Alpha and Omega, the beginning, and the ending, saith the Lord, which is, and which was, and which is to come, the Almighty," (Revelation 1:8). "Then one of the elders said to me, "Do not weep! See, the Lion of the tribe of Judah,

the Root of David, has triumphed. He is able to open the scroll and its seven seals," (Revelation 5:5).

The First Expose: Fear God

Upon our Lord and Savior, Christ Jesus' return, He will have occupied three positions of authority in three separate stages or phases of His eternal reign here on earth. The first has been completed, the second is in progress and the prophetic signs point to the third as imminent and looming. The truth that there is no fear of God among most of this current generation is why people are not mindful of our present conditions and times. Two thousand-plus years have passed, and just like humans do with the four postures of truth:

• Some accept His return,

• Others foolishly ignore and go on with their lives,

• Many deny the biblical Jesus or build their own Jesus and

• The Anti-Christs use government and false religion to murder the Truth (They have no fear, reverence, or belief in God).

Many Christians today, some knowingly, some unknowingly, are reluctant to get a proper perspective of the command to fear God. This concept is a stumbling stone for many of this age who profess to be walking upright yet have unresolved issues with heart disease easily identified by the lack of fruit of their work and deeds. You may ponder in your heart, "Why must we fear God; God is love, right?" This question can lead the natural man or the weak in faith to think God is harsh or cruel. Cruelty is far from the truth and not a part of God's character. What God is first and foremost, He is Holy. Two facets of God's Holy nature are sovereignty and truth. God says what He means and means what He says. God has allowed blessings and curses according to a man's ways by his choices alone to determine his eternal fate. Blessings lead to life and prosperity, whereas the curses' consequences lead to strife, destruction, and condemnation (Deuteronomy 11:26). God uses all things to complete His plans and purposes. The most brilliant man that ever lived, other than our Lord and Savior Jesus Christ, said, "There is a time and a season for everything under the sun," (Ecclesiastes 3:1). Listen, this might be the most important thing you have heard all day. No matter what path you choose in your life, in whatever the end, it will serve the purposes of God. Death and life, good and bad, blessings and curses all have places in God's eternal plans for a season. Whether you will be a judge of the unacceptable or a participant with the unacceptable, the choice is up to you (1 Corinthians 6:2). Many don't understand the will of God for His people and earth in this age of grace. The intention of God is not for a man to strive for lots of money, cars, houses, or an easy, trouble-free life at the expense of his neighbor. If a True Believer possesses many worldly riches, its purpose is first to do some Kingdom good works. Does God want you to have things? Yes! But God doesn't want things to have you! God in Christ takes pleasure in blessing His people with good gifts (Matthew 7:11). Let's prove it; the Holy Scriptures say, "Seek first the Kingdom of God, and its righteousness and all these other things will be added unto you (Matthew 6:33). Next, the Bible says, "Lay not up for yourselves treasures upon the earth where thieves steal and rust and moth corrupt, but build your treasure in heaven," (Matthew 6:19-20). Definitively James, the brother of Jesus, clarifies that the humble in circumstance should take pride in his high position, and the rich (what most of you want to be) will fade away like a wildflower (James 1:9-11). Finally, in a parable, Jesus said, "The cares of this world, the deceitfulness of riches, and the desire for other things choke out the Word of God in a man's heart, and it becomes unfruitful (Mark 4:19). So don't let what you thought you knew get in the way of what you don't know because of arrogance, pride, and offense. The revelation that you and I, and anyone else, are not who we thought we were is why the Lord had me write this book. We all on this road to sainthood are suffering the same way, just trying to get better each day. It takes all of us doing our assigned jobs to get there, and it will get better, *one day at a time*.

There is one concept the Lord talks about, makes references to, establishes, and makes covenants with His people from Genesis to Revelation. This concept is His relentless effort to create, establish, restore, and bless a family for Himself to reflect His presence on the earth as in heaven. When you understand God's family values, you can begin to know what His will is for you and all believers as His children. Understanding God's family values also help you understand His decisions in the Bible differently. The Bible repeats this theme throughout, "If you obey Me, you will be My people, and I will be your God," (Exodus 6:7). The fear of God becomes extremely important for us as children of God in these last days because, by covenant, the Lord said He would not leave us as orphans. A healthy fear of the Lord leads to knowledge, wisdom, and understanding. The fear of God serves two purposes: 1.) reverence for God as our Father, Creator, and Redeemer, and 2.) authority of God in and through all things.

True Believers have no excuse for not knowing God while having access to a fully completed Bible at their fingertips. People that don't believe have no reason as well. No one can say with a clear conscience that there is no God when all creation points directly to an Intelligent Designer and Orchestrator. Others who profess knowing God rehearse a verse or scripture reference and apply it out of context, mind you, to all their biblical studies simply because they refuse to accept the reality of the Kingdom of God. So many confess to being True Believers yet deny the invisible and natural spiritual war being fought daily between good and evil. The denial of the upcoming prophesied events will not change the plans of God but rather fulfill scripture as written from the foundations of the earth.

The Second Expose: Jesus 1.0 The Lamb of God

In the first century, God came to earth wrapped in human flesh and became the Lamb of God so that He may accrue our sins and allow all humankind the choice to live. Today, many professed believers are stuck on scripture references or out-of-context concepts because the truth Bible is too hard for some to bear. They are correct. For the natural man and carnal believers, the reality of the Gospel is terrifying. In a world where immorality, injustice, lawlessness, persecution, and oppression are at an astounding level, some are just waiting and wishing for some pre-2020 form of their old life to return. Many Christians deny the war constantly fought on earth between good and evil, the saints of God, the prince of the air, and his entourage of demons that wage war against them and all that is holy and of God in Christ Jesus. Some have suffered apathy in their faith walk toward their brothers and sisters in Christ Jesus and will try to enter heaven outside of genuine love for one another. Some are still unaware that everything connected to Jesus, the Lamb of God and Savior of the world, is grounded in love and non-negotiable.

The word *love*, meaning obedience to the teachings and commandments of Christ Jesus for all who accept Him as Lord and Savior, has primarily become carnal and flesh driven as opposed to the spiritual and loyalty commitment God seeks from His children (John 14:21).

So, this thought encourages the question of where Christ Jesus is today and what He is coming back to accomplish. God's preordained future is written, and disregarding the rough parts is dangerous to your eternity. In these future events, your participation or lack thereof will cement your place in eternity like it was written in the books from the earth's foundations. Many Christians today love the Lamb of God. It makes them feel good about themselves and their future when considering that this time on earth is increasingly becoming shorter and the reality of death inevitable.

Too many Christians in this generation overlook critical passages when confronted with the truth that the Lamb that died for the world's sins is the Lion of the Tribe of Judah and the Root of David (Revelation 5:5). The same Lamb of God will soon return to rule this earth with a rod of iron and pronounce judgment over all humanity. Heart disease has deceived many to ignore or skip those pages altogether conveniently.

The Bible speaks of the second coming of Christ in Revelation 19:11, and at this point, the period of grace has officially concluded, and Christ Jesus will embark on His third mission, which is the judgment of this earth. This second coming is precisely what John the Baptist said He would do in His earthly ministry, saying, "I indeed baptize you with water unto repentance, but one comes after me who shall baptize you with the Holy Spirit and fire," (Matthew 3:11-12).

The first earthly ministry of our Lord and Savior, Christ Jesus in the flesh, involved four specific works:

Redeem:

• Sent to the children of Israel first (Matthew 15:24)

• To save sinners (1 Timothy 1:12)

• To save the world (John 12:47)

• Kill the works of the devil (1 John 3:8)

• Be the propitiation for all humanity (Hebrews 2:1417)

• To be the Light of the world (John 12:46)

Regenerate:

• Reborn of water and Spirit (John 3:5)

• Transform the mind (Romans 12:2)

• Heart renewal (Jeremiah 31:31)

• Repentance for the remission of sins (Luke 3:3)

• Salvation (Romans 10:9-10)

• Sanctification (1 Thessalonians 5:23)

• Reconcile (Reconcile man to God)

• No condemnation for those in Christ Jesus (Romans 8:1)

• Tore the veil (Hebrews 10:20)

• Access to God (Ephesians 2:18)

• Come boldly to the throne of grace (Hebrews 4:6)

• Reconcile man to humanity

• No more Jew (Galatian 3:28)

• No more Greek (Galatian 3:28)

• No male (Galatian 3:28)

• No female (Galatian 3:28)

• No more enslaved person (Galatian 3:28)

• No more free, all equal (Galatian 3:28)

Restore:

• Peace (John 14:27)

• Life (John 10:10)

• Purpose (Jeremiah 29:11)

• Identity (Matthew 5:14)

• Influence (Matthew 5:13)

• Dominion (Matthew 5:5)

• Power (Acts 1:8)

• Holy Spirit (Acts John 14:26).

This list is not all-inclusive by far, for there are so many things that Christ Jesus accomplished in His three-and-a-half-year ministry. This list gives the reader an humbling realization of why Christ Jesus is not just our Savior but also our Lord. Achieving everything He was sent to accomplish as the Lamb of God, Christ Jesus cemented His earthly ministry by voluntarily shedding His innocent blood. This selfless act is why True Believers are responsible to the One who ensured our eternity and for everything He did for all humanity on the cross at Calvary. Completing His assignment ushered in the present and reigning authority, the Kingdom of God, through the person of the Holy Spirit, who does not

speak on His own but only reminds us of the things King
Jesus has said (John 16:13).

Jesus asked a question that is very relevant to the reception of
His message to the present world. Jesus said, "When I return,
will the Son of Man find faith on the earth?" (Luke 18:8).
Many statistics in America, the world's professed Christian
capital, indicate faith is severely declining. Only six in ten
Americans expect Jesus to return and judge everyone, and
fifty-six percent of believers deny a literal place called hell
where the unrighteous will be punished forever (Pew
Research Center). Statistic number three of the most
shocking church statistic data suggests that almost half of all
Americans have no idea, almost forty-four percent of where
they will go when they die, but only two percent believe that
they'll go to hell (American Worldview Inventory, Arizona
Christian University & Barna,). This data suggests a grim
disparity between the truth of the Gospel and the ignorance
of today's churches. Unfortunately, this data validates the
blatant indifference, denial, and deception that seeks to
endanger the witness of the True Church and its message of
salvation and light to the world. We will not prevail as True
Believers in our attempts to educate and expose people who
genuinely want to know the truth about their salvation if we
cannot find a way to introduce them to the truth. Man has

ignored God and Jesus, destroyed His earth, and the prophecies of the Bible are happening right before our very eyes.

The prophesied birth pains occurring on this earth are earthquakes, hurricanes, tsunamis, landslides, fires, famines, and pestilence. All these prophesied birth pangs are verifiable by doing a little research, but most don't know what they are looking for in all the information. Everything God made perfect the evilness and wickedness of man have perverted, and these are its consequences. Jesus gave a warning beforehand and assured all believers that these things must happen, so don't be afraid. However, the C4D5 chronic afflictions of humanity incite man to readily dismiss, ignore, or deny anything he doesn't accept or like. When Christ Jesus declared, "It is finished," it was a personal conversation between a Holy Son and His Holy Father signifying the completion of the work He performed. This statement marked the transition to the next phase of God's eternal plan for the world, you, me, and His Holy Spirit.

The Third Expose: Sitting at the Right Hand of the Father

Stage two, Jesus presently sits at the right hand of the Father. "Sit at my right hand until I place your enemies under your feet," (Matthew 22:44). A specific and necessary chain of events had to be completed for humankind to have an opportunity at salvation in these last days. If there is no Jesus, there is no cross, no cross, no blood, no blood, and then there is no death, no death, then no burial, no burial, and no resurrection to happen on the third day. Finally, if there is no resurrection, there is no ascension to Heaven fifty days later. No ascension means there is no descending of the Holy Spirit. No descending of the Holy Spirit catastrophically means there is no hope for the salvation of all humanity. Access to the Holy Spirit is a primary component of eternal life. None of these events, even remotely, are anything humans could do but depend upon the finished work of Christ Jesus alone. One of the provisions identified in The New Covenant is Jesus' life, death, and resurrection ushered in the age of the Holy Spirit in man. The finished work of Jesus manifested three prophetic events that God said He would do for his chosen people, the children of Israel, and what He would do for the world.

A.) There would be a descendant of the house of David forever on the throne of Israel. Jesus is the Son of Man born in the lineage of the house of David through the bloodline of His earthly father, Joseph, and mother, Mary. Jesus is the eternal Son of God, conceived by the Holy Spirit and of His virgin mother, Mary (Luke 1:30-35). The death of Jesus, being

117

sinless, dying for the sins of the entire world, and His subsequent resurrection, being the first risen from the dead to life eternal, qualifies Jesus by the power of God to be the ruler of the Kingdom of Heaven on earth.

B.) I will put my teachings within them and write them on their hearts. This covenant made by God superseded the first covenant, included the children of Israel, and covered the non-believing Gentiles that would come to believe later as well. God's covenant of grace opposed to the law that could not save, is predicated solely on belief in His Only sent Son. Christ Jesus commands believers to rely on God as their only provider, not this world that does not know God. When we accept Jesus as our Lord and Savior, our teacher, redeemer, King, and High Priest, we receive the gift of the Holy Spirit that acts in us like a conscience. He directs us into all things Jesus has said that protect us from our past, present, and future. His blood paid for all our sins, iniquities, and transgressions, which hijack our past and terrorize our thoughts of tomorrow. The Holy Ghost protects us from what we do in the future because we are sealed unto redemption until Christ Jesus returns for us, His enduring Church. We are also saved because we reside in Christ Jesus. He abides in us through knowing the Son of God, believing the Son of God, and repenting by doing the will of God found in His Word that cleanses us like water. People who are not a part of the church cannot receive the Holy Spirit. Therefore, they are in danger of condemnation at the expiration of their E³ART³H suit.

C.) The obedience of Jesus led to the age of grace. God forgave all iniquities and sins for all who believe. Jesus is now our High Priest in His established position at the Father's right hand, interceding to answer our prayers on our behalf. Jesus will remain at the position of the Father's right hand until all His enemies have been placed under his feet.

The bondage of the spiritually incarcerated lies in the refusal to turn the page from Jesus 1.0, the First-century Lamb of God, to the present 21st-century Lion of Judah. During this time, Christ Jesus returns as a King claiming His Kingdom and ruling the world as His Father commanded with a rod of iron. Jesus was obedient then, and He will do what His Father says to do through the power of the Holy Spirit when He returns. Jesus confessed that all He says and does is directly from God's mouth, making it righteous and valid. This truth fulfills the prophecy no one will need to teach you anything; God will teach all men through His Holy Spirit (John 6:45).

The Fourth Expose: The Lion of Judah

Stage three, our Lord and Savior, Jesus the Christ, will return to judge the entire world as the Lion of the Tribe of Judah and the Root of David. At a specified time that only God knows after everything the Bible says will happen up and unto that point, God will send the Son of Man back to the world to judge it, give every man his due reward, and retrieve His Church (Revelation 22:12). The root of David is on the brink of manifestation and could happen any day now. The Holy Scriptures say, "For judgment, I have come into this world so that those who do not see may see and that those who see may become blind," (John 9:39). Jesus is not talking to individuals who do not know God's good news of eternal life through trust in Him alone; no, these people had another problem. They suffered from heart disease. Despite overwhelming proof, they didn't believe He was the Messiah. These descendants of Abraham thought they understood the plan for eternal life but were blind to the truth that this Jesus, whom they denied, was the Only Way to the Father.

Like it or not, reject it, avoid it or not, but the Bible is clear that before Jesus returns, His enemies will be placed under His feet, and He will return to rule His Kingdom with an iron rod. Some professed believers who claim to be ready for the coming of the Lord are deceived just like they were in the days of Jesus. The Holy Scriptures speak of His return as hard to endure, difficult to stand, like a refiner's fire and laundered soap. The Bible says, "And He will sit as a refiner and purifier of silver; He will purify the sons of Levi and refine them like gold and silver. Then they will present offerings to the LORD in righteousness. 'And I will come near you for judgment; I will be a swift witness against sorcerers, against adulterers, against perjurers, against those who exploit wage earners and widows and orphans, and against those who turn away an alien— Because they do not fear Me,' says the LORD of hosts," (Malachi 3:2-5).

The prophet says on behalf of God, "I looked for anyone to repair the wall and stand in the gap for me on behalf of the land, so I wouldn't have to destroy it" (Ezekiel 22:30). Jesus 1.0 the Lamb, the lone Savior of the world, and Jesus 2.1 the Lion of Judah who fulfilled the gap. We must realize every single word that came out of the mouth of Jesus Christ was significant. Our Lord and Savior never spoke a word that did not have some principle, teaching, or example openly or hidden attached to it.

The biggest hurdle in today's church is possibly covered right in this chapter. The C4D5 chronic afflictions cause professed believers to readily dismiss, ignore, or deny anything they can't control, accept, or like.

121

What is certain is there is very little time left for grace, no more holding of hands, no extended conversations about what is right and wrong, and the time for courting is all but over. The Bible says of His mission, "He judges, and makes war with justice and righteousness," (Revelation 19:11). It is incredible that people who go to church every Sunday still don't realize that today's trials, tribulations, and testing are not by accident but by design. Jesus plainly outlined everything that would happen through the written word and assured us that these things must happen.

Envision the Promise: For you need endurance so that when you have done the will of God, you may receive what was promised (Hebrews 10:36)

KAP IT PRECEPT I THE CURRENCY OF THE KINGDOM OF GOD GMLP[3]

"Lay not up for yourselves treasures upon earth, where moth and rust doth corrupt, and where thieves break through and steal: But lay up for yourselves treasures in heaven, where neither moth nor rust doth corrupt, and where thieves do not break through nor steal:" (Matthew 6:19-20). "Grace be with you, mercy, and peace, from God the Father, and from the Lord Jesus Christ, the Son of the Father, in truth and love," (2 John 1:3).

The Bible says to "seek first the Kingdom of God, and all these other things will be added unto you," (Matthew 6:33). As explained in the introduction, the Kingdom of God is the authority of this age, a spiritual Kingdom influenced by the Holy Spirit living and working inside of every True Believer (John 14:17). So, likewise, the treasures we build up in heaven are not material but spiritual since nothing earthly and physical enters heaven (1 Timothy 6:7).

KAP IT precepts are Kingdom Alignment Principles and strategies for Implementation and Transformation that allow individuals to grow in their maturation and sanctification process in these last days. KAP IT precepts aid True Believers in their walk as tools for planning, building, and sanctifying their hearts and minds to the will of God. If you are a doctor, you heal for the Kingdom of God; if you are a lawyer, you represent people for the Kingdom of God; and likewise, in any profession that we do with the work of our hands, we do it to the glory and honor of the Kingdom of God (Colossians 3:17). In my vocation as a Human Resource Manager, the Word of God is my authority and the Holy Spirit, by the hand of God, is my witness that I write not in my name but in the name of Christ Jesus who sent me. How much Kingdom treasure have you invested in on this earth and saved up in heaven, where you will surely need it one day? This work will diligently remind you that you have a book in heaven with your name on it. Do you know what's in your book? Are there things in your book that you are unaware of or worse, things that were blotted out and disqualified because of the condition of your heart (Matthew 6:1)?

In the Kingdom, we do not like to use the word luck because we know God has His children in His hands, so we will say this is your blessed day! You no longer have to live your life as a broke Christian in the Spirit! Get yourself some spiritual currency that transcends this world and into the next! The Bible says, "You say I am rich. I have acquired wealth. I do not need a thing. But you do not realize that you are wretched, pitiful, poor, blind, and naked," (Revelation 3:17).

This quote has to be a misstatement, right? In this world and age of the church, if I am rich (worldly wealth), that has to be a sign from God that I am doing something right, and this is the fruit and blessings of my labor. Maybe, but are you sure? Another verse says, "Lay not up treasures for yourselves upon the earth, where moths and rust do corrupt, and where thieves break through and steal. But lay up for yourselves treasures in heaven where moths and rust do not corrupt. For where your treasure is there, your heart will also be," (Matthew 6:19-21). Ladies and gentlemen, can we then conclude that where your motivations, intentions, and opportunities are fixated, there is where your desires and love will also be? The last verse will make the picture even more transparent for some of you, and it goes back to where we started; the next verse (Revelation 3:18). The Bible says, "I counsel you to buy from me gold refined in the fire so you can become rich and white clothes to wear so you can cover your shameful nakedness. Finally, place a salve on your eyes so that you can see. Spiritually, gold refers to faith in Christ Jesus which the Bible says is more valuable than gold, tried and tested pure (1 Peter 1:7). White clothes refer to righteousness only found in Christ Jesus, whose unblemished, stainless, and blameless life and death cover our sinful souls when we believe in our hearts and confess Him alone as our Lord and Savior. Without His righteousness, we are naked and guilty of judgment (1 Corinthians 1:30). The spiritual eye salve we must apply involves keeping our eyes on Christ Jesus, the author, and finisher of our faith. He alone gives sight to the blind and blinds those who incorrectly see so perhaps they can see spiritually (John 9:39). Perhaps we, the church, have a priority problem because the doctrine of prosperity and self-promotion has dramatically overshadowed the biblical doctrines of selflessness and service. Riches in heaven are hardly the mindset of this new generation of the church. Everything revolves around God's will to prosper people first, with little or no emphasis on spiritual wealth, more often than not taught on Sundays regarding our finances and prosperity as children of the Most High God. Pastors, preachers, and teachers of this day and age speak with unmitigated authority that God's big plan for your life is that you have, if not all, most of the comfort and things money can buy, and this is the foundation of a good life. God does want you to have a prosperous life here. The Bible says it brings Him glory when worldly people see people of God prospering despite the setbacks, circumstances, and tumultuous situations life will throw at us from time to time (Deuteronomy 7:6-9). He doesn't want you to throw away your eternity at the expense of choosing the things God made instead of the Creator of the things! The prosperity gospel doctrines make for "good preaching, not good teaching," and we will get into that next section. Why, then, do we keep holding on to these teachings that do not help us find contentment in all things? Two significant reasons come to mind that I will discuss in this first Kingdom Alignment Precepts for Implementation & Transformation (KAP IT) principle of this book. Reason one is because we are not programmed that way because of our flesh nature, or more precisely, the C4D5 Chronic Affliction that we learned all humankind suffered after the fall from grace (Romans 5:12). We have discussed this phenomenon in detail over the first five chapters of this book and prayerfully understand that humanity is, for the most part, worse off now than ever before. The increase in knowledge has increased the pride in men, simultaneously increasing his already catastrophic rebellion, disobedience, and lawlessness (2 Timothy 3:1-5). The second reason is that at that time, we didn't fully understand the mystery of the Kingdom of God and His righteousness and the command by Christ Jesus to seek this first above all things (Matthew 6:33).

Every kingdom has some monetary currency that allows you to buy, sell, and trade goods and services to support that kingdom's economy and government. The Kingdom of God is a Spiritual Kingdom that requires spiritual currency. **Again, The Kingdom of God is God's accepted, and man's**

approved spiritual will of joy, peace, and righteousness in the Holy Spirit, reflected through His church on this earth, that gives the power to influence whosoever wills character (thoughts, attitudes, and behaviors) in service to Christ Jesus. Gold and silver are universal currencies used throughout history and are considered two of the world's most valuable precious metals. The Bible uses gold and silver as metaphors for the judgments of God that are true, righteous, and in comparison, sweeter than honey to him who receives it (Psalms 19:9-10).

Only one Kingdom has a currency whose value transcends time and eternity and is more widely accepted than Visa, Master Card, or American Express combined. This Kingdom's currency has no boundaries and is accepted in courtrooms, hospitals, and between family, friends, and your enemies, too. Unlike worldly money, this currency has no limitations and is available to all nationalities, ethnic groups, and cultures, regardless of socioeconomic status or political affiliation. This currency I am referring to is called the Grace of God, Mercy of God, Love of God, and the Peace OF God, WITH God, and IN God (GMLP^3), only found in Christ Jesus. Six is the number of man, and if a man is to transition from this life to the next and not suffer loss, he must at some point invest in these six stock options while he is still on the earth (1 Corinthians 3:12-15).

Grace of God. The grace of God is the method the Lord used to change the heart of stone in a man to a heart of flesh he can use. Grace, the gift from God that cleansed all man's unrighteousness, gave humanity the motivation through faith; we receive right standing with God in Jesus Christ. The New Covenant says I will forgive their iniquity and remember their sins no more (Jeremiah 31:31). Further, so that no man can boast, it is by grace we have been saved through faith, not of works (Ephesians 2:8). Grace is the motivation to live out the commandments of God daily. With the proper understanding of who we are, we can grasp the magnitude of the gift of grace afforded to us as fallen human beings, the grace of God found in Christ Jesus, who loved us first and gave His sinless life for our sinful life. We have the courage and perseverance through the Holy Spirit given to us as a promise of our salvation, assurance that we already have the victory.

Mercy of God. The mercy of God, used hand in hand with the grace of God as the currency of the Kingdom, also affords us the intention to serve unto God and in Christ Jesus. God's heart and intention are to forgive anyone who repents. Mercy has been depicted as the favor of God not to give us the punishment we rightly deserve. Grace, then, is the favor of

God that provides us with what we don't deserve. The Bible says, "If we confess our sins, the Father is faithful and just to forgive," (1 John 1:9). He saved us not based on deeds done in righteousness, but according to his mercy, by the washing, regeneration, and renewing of man's spirit with the Holy Spirit (Titus 3-5).

Love of God. It's all about love, which is the summation of God's grace, mercy, and peace that He has afforded us rest in His steadfast love for his children and this world. The love of God is a two-way street: His love for us first and our reciprocal love for our Father in Christ Jesus, who redeemed and saved us. All things are grounded in love, and love is the intention God used to complete His master plan. The Bible says, "For God so loved the world that He gave His only begotten Son, that whosoever believed in Him should not perish but have everlasting life," (John 3:16). There has never been an act of love that will ever rival Christ Jesus's love for humanity (John 15:13). God instilled this love in Him who showed His love for us first, that while we were yet sinners, He sent Jesus to save us (Romans 5:8).

Peace of God (OWI Peace). The peace of God is the currency of the Kingdom that satisfies our last heart problem, the opportunity to serve God in Christ Jesus. This peace is not the peace the world gives that is here today and gone tomorrow, but a peace that is living and working in you. The finished work on the cross by our Lord and Savior Christ Jesus satisfied the debt all humanity owed. Now those in Christ Jesus have peace, reconciled unto God and man. We, unlike the world, do not have the anxiety incurred by the fear of death of this EARTH suit because we believe in Christ Jesus and have rest for our souls.

In the south, we grew up using the colloquial phrase "owee," which meant something was over the top, really good, or as an exclamation point, for example, "owee, did you see that"? It was fitting when we inserted the acronym "OWI" to describe a peace that is truly over the top and unmatched by any emotional contentment one could ever imagine, that the parallel could be easily grasped by those familiar with southern culture.

The OWI peace *Of* God is a total contentment that covers the emotional state we have of God that comforts us in times of trouble, hard times, and trials that keeps the True Believer from submitting to fear. We know God is with us and will protect us during these times. This peace surpasses all understanding and guards our hearts and minds in Christ Jesus (Philippians 4:7). Let the Peace of God rule your hearts in which you were called to one body (Colossians 3:15).

The OWI peace *With* God is the peace of mind True Believers have with God because Christ Jesus, by the finished work on the cross, has satisfied the debt of death caused by our sins. The death of our Lord and Savior, Christ Jesus, reconciled us to God and man once and for all time (Hebrews 7:27) . Justified by our faith in Him alone as the Son of God raised from the dead, we are counted as righteous before God our Father, which surpasses all understanding and will guard our hearts and minds in Christ Jesus (Philippians 4:7). Therefore, having been justified by faith, we have PEACE WITH GOD through our Lord Jesus Christ (Romans 5:1).

The OWI peace *In* God is the peace that dwells and manifests itself in True Believers because we abide in Christ Jesus. When the True Believer crucifies his fleshly nature and crucifies worldly desires and passions, he has accepted Christ Jesus (Galatians 5:16). Having spiritually died with Him, we have faith that God hears our prayers, knows our needs and desires, and will do them according to His will. The Bible says "I have been crucified with Christ; it is no longer I who live, but Christ lives in me; and the life which I now live in the flesh I live by faith in the Son of God, who loved me and gave Himself for me," (Galatians 2:20). You keep him IN perfect peace whose mind stays on you because He trusts you (Isaiah 26:3).

Envision the Promise: Grace, mercy, and peace from God our Father and Jesus Christ our Lord (1 Timothy 1:2)

Good Preaching Not Good Teaching

But there were also false prophets among the people, just as there will be false teachers among you. They will secretly introduce destructive heresies, even denying the sovereign Lord who bought them--bringing swift destruction on themselves (2 Peter 2:2). For the time is coming when people will not endure sound teaching, but having itching ears, they will accumulate for themselves teachers to suit their own passions and will turn away from listening to the truth and wander off into myths (2 Timothy 4:3).

The First Expose: Good Preaching

In a world where most are led primarily by sensual, natural feelings, limited understanding, selfish desires, and needs, we can understand why Jesus told Peter, "Get thee behind Me, Satan; you are an offense to me!" Peter, who, just minutes before, had just made a remarkable observation Jesus himself said could only have been revealed from God, is now the devil! The problem Peter had, and what Christians worldwide still struggle with today, is discerning and mixing the spiritual will of God versus our natural will and desires for our lives. Christ Jesus emphasized the only way we receive the Kingdom of God, which is one hundred percent spiritual (1 Corinthians 15:50), is to be reborn of water and the Spirit (John 3:5). Spiritual rebirth has three stages. The Bible says, and such were some of you, but you were washed, but you were sanctified, but you were justified in the name of the Lord Jesus and by the Spirit of God (1 Corinthians 6:11).

1) Washed

- Belief that the Word of God cleanses us from all unrighteousness (Ephesians 5:26)
- Washed through baptism through the Holy Spirit into one body (Acts 22:16)
- Washed through baptism in Christ Jesus in His death, we also died to sin (Romans 6:3)
- Washed by the blood (1 John 1:7)
- Baptized into Christ Jesus as our garment of righteousness (Galatians 3:27)

2) Sanctified

- Sanctified by His word, sanctified by His truth (John 17:16)
- Sanctified by the blood of Christ Jesus (Hebrews 13:12)
- Sanctified through God Himself (Thessalonians 5:23)
- Sanctified through the body of Jesus (Hebrews 10:10)
- Sanctified by the finished work of the cross (Hebrews 10:14)
- Sanctified by grace (Acts 20:32)

3) Justified

- But to him that does not work but believes on Him that justifies the ungodly his faith is accounted for righteousness (Romans 4:5)

- Justified not by works, not of anything we could have done (Romans 3:28)
- Justified by the Holy Spirit (Romans 8:16)

Through faith in Jesus, the Word of God, when we obey His teaching and live by His example, which gives light, we are counted as in Him, cleansed and righteous. This result stems from His obedience to God, who sent Him to the cross to shed His innocent blood that washes away our sins so that everyone who believes in Him might be saved (John 3:16). A person must believe unto righteousness in Christ Jesus as the Son of God and the only acceptable access to the Father. The term unto righteousness means we acknowledge our sinful nature and choose to crucify it on the cross as Christ Jesus did for His True Church (Romans 6:6). The belief in one's heart (intentions, motivations, and opportunities) means accepting Christ Jesus as Lord over your life (Romans 10: 910). The Bible requires us, as children of God, to be perfect as He is perfect (Matthew 5:48). The only person that has

ever walked this earth perfect and approved by God is the Son of Man, Christ Jesus. We are counted as perfect when we live according to his will. Sanctification means we are now set apart from unbelievers. You must deny your old unacceptable worldly and fleshly living and worldview and seek the holy and acceptable Christ-centered worldview available in and through the Holy Spirit. This new life consists of daily repentance of whatever is unacceptable to God, called sin. A principle of life that is made aware here is what this ministry coins as the Kingdom principle of exposure. The Kingdom principle of exposure states once you have been exposed to anything, you cannot be unexposed. Once exposed, you must, at some moment, make a conscious decision of how to channel and handle the information, situation, or circumstance moving forward. Spiritually speaking, purification, rebirth, and death are the only ways to be unexposed to anything. Here is an example of each.

- Information -- If I had not come and spoken to them, they would have no sin, but now they have no excuse for their sin (John 9:41)
- Situation -- But you must not eat of the tree of the knowledge of good and evil, for in the day that you do, you will surely die (Genesis 2:17)
- Circumstances -- Therefore, just as through one man sin entered the world, and death through sin, and thus death spread to all men because all sinned (Romans 5:12) Physical Contact Furthermore, anything that the

unclean person touches shall be unclean; and the person who touches it shall be unclean until evening (Numbers 19:22).

The Kingdom of God, law of exposure, is seen clearly in the Garden of Eden with the information revealed to the first man Adam. This cleansing process stipulating abstinence, water/blood washing, removal of the unclean thing, and a waiting period has been the purification method God has used to this very age. After being forewarned that eating the forbidden fruit would result in death, Adam ate it anyway. "The man has become like us, knowing good and evil, so he was banished from the garden before he could eat of the tree of Eternal life and live forever," (Genesis 3:22-24). We now know through our previous chapters that our mental conditioning and corresponding human disposition are naturally contrary to the will of God for our lives. So, had man eaten of the tree of Eternal life in his current sinful condition, he would forever be cursed to live in a corrupted natural body. God then killed an animal, made some clothes for them, pronounced judgment and curses on all parties involved, and then proceeded to banish them from the garden, promising they would eventually die. The killing of the animal and banishment forever from the Garden of Eden fulfilled the last two requirements: blood/water cleansing and abstinence.

When we are motivated and led by our feelings and emotions, they direct us, sometimes knowingly and other times unknowingly and prematurely, toward things looking or sounding like the perceived will and Word of God but ultimately coincide with our flesh-driven desires and livelihood. The Holy Scriptures say there is a way that seems right to a man, but its end is death (Proverbs 14:12). Continuing unchecked in this emotionally biased worldview inevitably causes one to accept the false teaching that the listener may receive as doctrine.

The cares of life have created an earthly playground of evil and wickedness for charismatic individuals teaching in pulpits, podcasts, YouTube channels, and even in today's churches. Jesus said to practice and observe whatever they tell you, but don't follow their examples, for they don't practice what they teach (Matthew 23:3). There are many examples of what the church is not supposed to look like and should not be focused upon these last days. Unfortunately, the good ones get a bad rap when they merely try to give people the truth of the gospel.

As prophesied, the falling away of people from the True Church grows increasingly prevalent the closer to the Day of

Christ Jesus. Churchgoers professing themselves as True Believers won't admit it, but the numbers do not lie as people tend to do. Statistics show a dramatic decline in attendance, dropping to levels never seen before. Many people who confess salvation have little or no understanding of fundamental Biblical doctrine and beliefs. And that's okay! That's not the issue. A follower of the Lord Christ Jesus does not need to be a theology major or biblical scholar, and you don't have to be a historian or a linguist in Arabic, Hebrew, or Greek. The only qualifications a person must have to be a follower of Christ Jesus are commitment and faith. The problem, however, is three-fold:

1). People will not discern what is biblically right or wrong in the eyes of God. Not right in your mother's eyes, friend's eyes, supervisor's eyes, or even the president's eyes, but aligned with God's word. Jesus asked this same question why cannot you discern for yourselves what is right?

2). The word has been subjected to ambiguity and manipulation by those who interpret it for their selfish gain. The line between acceptable and unacceptable in the Kingdom of God has been blurred for some time, recognizing the defiled, abominable, and evil as acceptable and presenting a false gospel to this thirsty generation.

3). We have said this many times; many still don't believe God is who He says He is and will do what He says he will do.

Church affiliation is rapidly declining among the generations that succeed the baby boomers and Generation X. Steadily diluted and polluted by worldly and manufactured principles, the gospel spirals into precisely what our Lord, the prophets, and apostles prophesied. Having been forewarned through years of Bible prophecy, it is not surprising that His elect, the church, will be overwhelmed by lawlessness. Preaching the flip side of the good news, especially to this generation, is a monumental task. Downplayed in some churches today is obedience to Christ Jesus and replaced with strictly the prosperity sections of the Word of God, and others avoid preaching the consequences entirely. The belief in and commands of Christ Jesus are the essential and foundational aspects of the Christian faith by which we attain our salvation and sanctification. No amount of money or the abundance of material wealth can save your soul or pay your way out of the SPA (Satan's permanent abode). Through the Holy Spirit, we have the grace and mercy of God to repent and keep His commands through the belief that Jesus the Christ satisfied what we could not do on our own. Jesus did not abolish the law or the prophets; He came and fulfilled the law because we would never be able to oblige this task.

Once we believe and trust in Christ Jesus alone, there is an extensive amount of submission, sacrifice, faith, sanctification, and that word that most humans are allergic to, "suffering," to make us battle-ready, tested, and mature believers needing nothing. Preachers have designed their ministry to keep the chairs filled instead of filling the hearts of the children of God with truth, righteousness, and the conviction of the Holy Spirit. Some knowingly and some not, many are more motivated by the control, power, and perks of preaching here in this 21st century, and it is showing up in the lack of self-control, faith, perseverance, and sincere love on behalf of the Believer that compromises the church's purpose and legitimacy.

So, what do we need to look for when seeking a faithful shepherd for our souls? Let us start by identifying the habits of teachers and preachers Christ Jesus told us we should beware of in Matthew twenty-three.

•They crush people with unbearable religious demands and never lift a finger to ease the burden

•They do their work to be seen by men

•They seek honor and special treatment

- They preach tithes and offerings religiously while neglecting more important things like justice, mercy, faith, belief, and judgment

- Conflicting unbiblical gospel messages

- Once saved, always saved with no conditions

The Second Expose: Examples

The last iconic words spoken by our Lord and Savior in his earthly bodily ministry is one of the most preached, misused, and misappropriated scripture references that reflect our commemoration of Resurrection Sunday, entitled "It Is Finished." The church of this age uses this scripture reference to imply that we have nothing to do morally or civilly because the death on the cross of our Lord and Savior completely satisfied the debt existing between God and man restoring him to his rightful place. However, this is true, but not the end of the story. "It is finished" was a personal conversation between The Father and His One and only Son completing His assignment in His earthly body (John 17:4). The work completed was humanity had been spiritually restored to our original position as kings with dominion and rulership over everything on the earth, including the devil, while at the same time having God in and among us in fellowship forever (Hebrews 5:9). This statement is correct. But there is a flip side to this equation. You were bought with a price. You are either a slave of righteousness or a slave of sin, and there is no middle ground (Romans 6:16). Nothing you have or own could free you from death because of the C4D5 Chronic Affliction that separates you from a Holy God. The only suitable substitute for the redemption of sins is the blood (Hebrews 9:22), acceptable to God from an unblemished and holy replacement. This suitable replacement, my friends, is only found in One Person who has ever walked this earth, our Lord and Savior Christ Jesus, who died for the entire world's sins! Glory to God! Thank You, Lord Jesus! This teaching, "It's Finished," and ones like it slowly and methodically cause believers to follow man-made doctrines instead of the inerrant Word of God presented in the written Bible.

Futility is the ignorant and foolish act of doing something over and over again, gaining nothing in return each time. The denial of something does not make the truth of it go away. Refusing to trust, believe, and obey the Word of God does not change the mind or the will of God for your life. Futility reinforces His will for the righteous who avoid judgment because they heeded and obeyed the Word of God, which is the truth! The Bible says I am the Lord your God I do not change, and this is why you are not consumed, (Malachi 3:6) and another place, Jesus is the same yesterday, today, and forever (Hebrews 13:8).

The Third Expose: Good Teaching

Not having a healthy, honest, and accurate worldview of who God is, what His plans are, and what He ultimately requires of you will lead one down the road of inevitable, repetitious deception. Whether self-inflicted or at the hands of the enemy (divinations), you tend to live a life of inconsistency and defeat. After much wasted time, you will discover and find yourself working against the plans of God for your life instead of with God to accomplish them (futility). The book of knowledge says, "What does the Lord require of you than to act justly toward others, show mercy as I have shown mercy to you, and to walk humbly with your God" (Micah 6:8). This verse poses a problem for affected individuals who have not fully surrendered to the sovereignty of God. What happens as it always has, people start to run astray and put words into God's mouth that He neither said nor told them to say. The character and will of God never change, but the flip side of that equation is that He sometimes changes His methods to accomplish His perfect will. For example, because it would be impossible for man in his current fallen state to fully meet all the requirements of the holiness God requires for His children, God enacted a masterful plan that included the sacrifice of His One and Only Son. This plan would satisfy God's righteousness, objectives, and will for His people once and for eternity.

With the prophesied increase of technology, lawlessness, and the predisposition to operate in one's own will, the world and some in the church are also failing. The disregard for acting justly with one's neighbors, creating cycles of poverty for individual races, and total neglect for the holiness of God requires of His children has propelled man into a bottomless abyss in which only calling on the name of the Lord will repair.

The following five-chapter dig at the root of these problems beginning with where these divinations and the futility that afflicted individuals are operating come from. Then we will discuss the issues of the institution created to stop the very thing that has overtaken the world of believers today. Inside the institution, known as the church, there has been infiltration of what the Book of Knowledge calls Gentiles, who have brought their own beliefs, values, and culture and built their religion. We must acknowledge and diffuse the teaching that has allowed this generation of believers to operate unchallenged in error due to their misunderstanding, ignorance, or rejection of the clearly stated grace, mercy, and love of God in Christ Jesus and through the power of the Holy Spirit. Next, we will break down one of the New Testament's most controversial and broadly disputed doctrines, which outlines the quickest and surest way to hell, blasphemy against the Holy Spirit, our witness. Finally, this section will end with a depiction that hopefully sets a sense of urgency inside your spirit to know precisely where we are on this timeline called life on earth.

Envision the Promise: Be diligent to present yourself approved to God, a worker who does not need to be ashamed, rightly dividing the word of truth (2 Timothy 2:15).

Chapter Six

THAT THING BEFORE THE CHURCH

"And I also say unto thee, that thou art Peter, and upon this rock, I will build my church; and the gates of hell shall not prevail against it," (Matthew 16:18). "There is one body and one Spirit, just as you were called in one hope of your calling; one Lord, one faith, one baptism; one God and Father of all, who is above all, and through all, and in you all," (Ephesians 4:4-6). And He put all things under His feet and gave Him to be head over all things to the church, which is His body, the fullness of Him who fills all in all," (Ephesians 1:22-23). So we, being many, are one body in Christ, and individually members of one another," (Romans 12:5).

The First Expose: My Church

This scripture reference is given in Matthew 16:18, quoting Christ Jesus stating, "Upon this rock, I will build my church, and the gates of hell will not prevail against it," is the foundation of the New Testament church. Given at the inception of what is known today as it was two thousand years ago, as the called-out people, the followers of Christ Jesus, whom He would self-identify this group as His church. "My church fulfills the prophecy God made to establish a

Kingdom of priests for His very own and Holy unto Him,"
(Revelation 1:6). Never in the history of the world will there be
such a collection of diverse groups of individuals based solely
on one criterion, belief in the One and Only Son of God.
Despite all that humanity and the accuser of the brethren will
do to preclude, conclude, and exclude discipleship, precisely as
it was written, the church has throughout history and will
continue to prevail.

This chapter entitled "That thing before the church" speaks
to the disconnect between Christ Jesus's church and the
church body that we see prevalent today. Over time, the
"True Church," the one Jesus established, has been gradually
compromised and changed to reflect worldly flesh-centered
thoughts, desires, and behaviors. The false church was built
devoid of the laws and commands of Christ Jesus but on
sensuality, feelings, emotions, and human wisdom. A healthy
fear of God and a wake-up call of the lack of time left is
necessary to get back to the original purpose and function of
the church Christ Jesus established. The perpetual condition
of man's heart is the how, when, and where problems and
things went wrong for the body of the church. The church's
problem today is that not enough seek to get it right.
Everyone wants to be right about their individual and shared

beliefs, even at the expense of perverting the gospel and misinterpreting the doctrine of God in Christ Jesus.

The Second Expose: Not Your Church

The church was created for and belongs to Christ Jesus. Contrary to many popular beliefs, our salvation is not about you! We in this EARTH suit are not so good, loving, or faithful that we deserve a Righteous and all-powerful God to send His Sinless Son to die in our place. If we were truly as smart as we propose, we would fall on our knees more often and ask the Good Lord to pity us because truthful people understand we are an utter mess. Undoubtedly, if you are breathing now or anyone who has ever lived whose blood ran warm through their veins, salvation includes you most definitely, but not about your goodness, work, or will. Salvation comes through One God-Man, Christ Jesus. For the believer, as sure as you will live and not die, purchased by the blood, the Church Christ Jesus built for His servants will prevail through all eternity (Revelation 21:4). There is only One "True Church" for "True Believers," as it is one Lord, one faith, one baptism, and one God of all, overall, and in all (Ephesians 4:4-5). Period. The called-out group of individuals is referred to in the Holy Scriptures as those who endure to the end. This True Church is a collection of God's children in Christ Jesus throughout time who love Him and accepted

Him as Lord and Savior. The Catholic, Lutheran, Methodist, Southern Baptist, and all the thousands of churches like them have all contributed knowingly or unknowingly to the present divide in the body of Christ Jesus. The loss of biblical knowledge and influence the church has suffered in the sight and presence of the very people Jesus has sent us to witness is nothing short of catastrophic. The bickering, fighting, and backbiting, not to mention the total disregard for fundamental biblical doctrine, will have far-reaching consequences on the professed leaders of this age. There has been little effort among the mega-churches to preach and teach the necessity of the church's unity these last days. Even among the best teachers and preachers today, very few transcend the racial, ethnic, denominational, political, or socio-economic barriers that circumvent the oneness of mind of today's churches.

The Third Expose: My Jonas Experience -- Jonas is a biblical prophet that had a problem with the nation of Nineveh, people he didn't care for very much because of their cruel nature and the fact that they were Gentiles or people that did not honor God. God, however, sent Jonas to preach to them to repent or suffer the same fate as Sodom and Gomorrah years prior in the days of Lot (Genesis 14:12). I particularly sympathize with this story of Jonas because, for me, the people I wanted to avoid were the modern-day church folk. Some of the most arrogant, unforgiving, judgmental, and unloving people I have ever met have called themselves Christians. I genuinely have felt more love connected to my called demographics: the incarcerated, homeless, poor, disabled veterans, and people of a wayward lifestyle than some of my Christian colleagues. These afflicted individuals welcome and appreciate a life change more than I wanted to write "to know it all" Christians who lacked, above all things love. And even for those who didn't receive the word or the Christian worldview, it was understandable because they have never had exposure as some believers claim to possess.

As it happened one night, I was writing this book, and I noticed the writing gearing more and more toward today's church challenges more than toward the people I assumed my assignment was to help. So, my question to the Lord that night was, "Are we trying to change the church?" The Spirit spoke to me immediately with three observations that I will never forget, and it changed my Jonas perspective entirely. The first observation stated there is nothing wrong with the church. "I (Christ Jesus) created the church, and the church is perfect." Second observation, "Which church are you referring to, because there are seven of them, and only one is acceptable to God?" In a later chapter, we will discuss the names of the types of churches in detail. Finally, the Spirit's last statement prompted this chapter; there is nothing wrong with the church; it is the thing before the church that has caused the identity crisis, loss of influence, and power. I later understood this concept more clearly by reflecting on my younger days in the church where I grew up in a Methodist denomination. I remembered The Apostle's Creed, a dedication or affirmation of faith read and spoken aloud to confirm religion and belief. As I was reciting the creed, everything was fine and in agreement until I got to the part that said, "I believe in the holy Catholic Church." Bingo, that was it. Exactly! Catholic before the church, Methodist before the church, and Baptist before the church creating "the thing before the church." What has been done over generations by man and by the enemy's design is to gradually and seamlessly make the church secondary and subordinate to the thing that comes before it. We have participated unknowingly in culture, rituals, and traditions that have subconsciously or fearfully contributed to the demise of the very thing we say we seek to create, which is church unity under One God in Christ Jesus and through the power of the Holy Spirit. We have not become one Church under Jesus at many locations; we have become many self and culture-identified churches worldwide.

A better understanding of the Kingdom of God, coupled with not focusing on many different parts but the "Church"

as one body, is the key to restoring identity, influence, and power to today's churches.

A). Identity. The identity of the overcoming church is the likeness and image of our Lord and Savior, Christ Jesus. This lacking characteristic is evidence of significant problems in the 21st-century church. There is no confusion about who Jesus is, what He came to do, or how he lived His earthly life. What is confusing is consistency and written documentation are available and used by all churches, yet there is still a disconnect. The problem is the churches have become cultural, ethnic, and religious icons conforming to the likeness and taste of their leaders. The new-age church division is a by-product of years and years of the gradual C4D5 chronic conditioning that has detracted from man's relationship with the Holy Spirit and His Lord and Savior.

B). Influence. People choose and attend churches similarly to sporting events, entertainment venues, or postsecondary schools. I'm a member of this church, or we do it this way, or we do it that way. This state of mind for the modern-day church has caught up with them and is now out of control. At the point where the church's size, name, and race of people attending the church became more important than the church's mission, we failed. Am I suggesting changing the names of all the churches? No, but I am saying that we have to change the mindset, culture, and direction of this current church if we, in any way, shape, or form, can begin to prepare for the trials and testing that are currently upon us and the sure hell on earth if not in our lifetime, our children's.

C). Power. To regain the first-century churches' power and authority, we must make some tough choices that most are not prepared to make. The Bible says the Lord does not dwell in temples made with human hands (Acts 7:48). Where did it go so wrong that believers started worshipping the building instead of the builder? This premise is the foundation of this argument about the condition of the modern-day, 21st Century Church and was echoed by our Lord and Savior two thousand years ago as he rebuked the heart (motives, intentions, and opportunity) of the religious leaders of that day. Christ Jesus confronted the Pharisees and Sadducees for their hypocrisy, corruption, greed, pride, and biased interpretation of righteousness without fruit-filled evidence, overshadowing their outward appearance of commitment and dedication to God and His law (Matthew 23:1-36). This ideology later crept into the first-century church as some tried to preach their gospel instead of the only gospel, Christ Jesus, crucified for our sins. The Bible is clear that to sit on the throne with Jesus in the world to come, just as Jesus overcame and now sits at Father's right hand, we must do the same (Revelation 3:21). The things we unknowingly place in front of the "One" established church called the "overcoming church" of Christ Jesus has caused us to be precisely what the Apostle Paul warned us of in 1 Corinthians 3:1-16. The Bible tells us that wherever there is strife, envy, and division, we are operating not of the Spirit but carnal, man-influenced doctrines and behaviors (James 3:16). The current number of Christian denominations in the United States alone is at least two hundred, more than forty-five thousand worldwide. This data suggests we have gone from bad to worse. Several things must begin to occur before Christ Jesus returns for His bride, the church. First, the church must draw a line between worldly wisdom and the wisdom of God, one or the other. Christ Jesus said to be hot or cold; he spews out the lukewarm. Second, each must adopt a personal commitment to the Kingdom of God here on earth and plant it in the hearts of people who profess themselves as the True Church. Third, speak the truth in love, preach and teach the gospel and bear the cross prepared for us, the called disciples of Christ Jesus.

The Fourth Expose: The Overcoming Church -- the Church that Jesus created and will return for has only one characteristic that only a hand full of present-day churches endorses. That characteristic is its commitment to overcoming unto the end (Revelation 3:21). Being adequately forewarned of the perils and trials that precede our Lord and Savior's imminent return, it is our responsibility to each be a rock in the body of Christ Jesus, which is the True Church.

Undoubtedly, the groundwork for the final battle, the new world order, has officially been ushered in. The only thing that stands between countless lives lost to sin, rebellion, and disobedience is the True Church performing the duties commanded to us to accomplish. "Go into all the world, make disciples of all nations, baptizing them in the name of the Father, the Son, and the Holy Spirit, and teaching them to obey all I have commanded you (Matthew 28:19-20).

Church PPE (Personal Protective Equipment) We have stated the identity of the church resides in our Lord and Savior, Christ Jesus who

- Always glorified God

- Lived a sinless life

- Endured the cross

- Defeated the grave, death, and hell

- Finished the work set before Him from the foundations of the earth

If we profess ourselves as the chosen, we are predestined, called, justified, and glorified to complete good works (Romans 8:29-31). To effectively accomplish this mission, we need the Holy Spirit's power to help in areas where we lack natural ability and wisdom. We need our spiritual, personal protective equipment. This equipment given to the saints through the Spirit is not optional but mandatory and essential to have a seat at the Marriage Supper of the Lamb (Revelation 19:9). The righteous acts of the saints dressed in fine linen (Revelation 19:8) at the wedding are the ones who possess

- Patience: Those who keep the commandments of God and the faith of Jesus (Revelation 14:12)

- Perseverance: Because you have kept My command to persevere, I will keep you from the hour of testing (Revelation 3:10)

- Endurance: He who endures to the end will be saved (Matthew 24:13).

We understand that we can't change everybody and that everybody doesn't want to be changed, no matter how much they know. People will still go to the church instead of being the True Church until Jesus comes and sets everything in order. Until then, what we must do in these last days is get our own houses in order, protect, share, and hold fast to what we have in the truth of the gospel with everyone the Lord sends us to minister to, one person at a time.

Envision the Promise: But now, O' Lord, You are the Father, we are the clay, you are our Potter, and all of us are the works of Your hand (Isaiah 64:8).

Chapter Seven
GENTILES HIDING BEHIND A CROSS

"Therefore, do not worry, saying, 'What shall we eat?' or 'What shall we drink?' or 'What shall we wear?' 32 For after all these things the Gentiles seek," (Matthew 6:31-32). "Not everyone who says to me, 'Lord, Lord,' will enter the Kingdom of heaven, but the one who does the will of my Father who is in heaven. On that day, many will say to me, 'Lord, Lord, did we not prophesy in your name, and cast out demons in your name, and do many mighty works in your name?' And then will I declare to them, 'I never knew you; depart from me, you workers of lawlessness," (Matthew 7:21-23). "These people draw near to Me with their mouth and honor Me with their lips, but their heart is far from Me. And in vain they worship Me, Teaching as doctrines the commandments of men," (Matthew 15:8-9). "And he that taketh not his cross and followed after me is not worthy of me," (Matthew 10:38).

The First Expose: Jew or Gentile?

As we alluded to before, there are only two types of people in the eyes of the Lord; the saved called his True Church, and the unsaved, whom He refers to as the Gentiles. After your dirt nap, there is only one of two possible places you will call home once you have departed from this EARTH suit, either with God in eternity or away from God in hell in eternity. The Bible says in the last days, "I will separate on my right the sheep, referring to the saved, and on my left the goats, the unsaved," (Matthew 25:31-46). The Jewish nation, the original children of God and benefactors of God's eternal covenant through their forefather Abraham, paved the way for the world's salvation. We, the church, who are not Jews by birth, have been adopted into the fold by faith in Christ Jesus, who died for the entire world's sins. The present-day church and the first-century Jews suffered from the same prevalent problem, their heart condition. Jesus said, "You honor me with your lips, but your hearts are far from me." Isaiah prophesied this scripture seven hundred and thirty years before Jesus quoted it to the Jewish nation. It still reigns true even more powerfully two thousand years later. We know, from reading the Bible, that lip service was prevalent in that era and continues today. The Jewish nation, the children of the promise, have forsaken their vow to the Lord, refused to repent of their ways, denied the Son of God, and by default, have opened the door for the entire world to be partakers of salvation. Once exclusive to only the Hebrew nation and their servants (Romans 11:11), this salvation is now available to the world through grace by faith. Our Christ Jesus' people, because of the hardness of their hearts, followed Jesus for three and a half years, partaking of all His miracles, signs, and wonders, only to betray him literally to the death. After three years of preaching salvation, healing the blind, sick, afflicted, casting out demons, and in one week, the tables turned to a repulsive and morbid sequence of events. These events included Palm Sunday, Hosanna to the King, clearing the temple on Monday, the fig tree judgment on Tuesday, and the Last Supper on Thursday. Finally, they asked Pilate for the thief and murderer, Barabbas, and then crucified our Lord and Savior on Friday for the finale. But thank God that was not the end of the story! Three days later, He rose from the dead and now sits at the Father's right hand, where he shall judge the quick and the dead (Christian Classics Ethereal Library).

The Second Expose: Bear Your Cross Daily

Jesus bared the cross meant for us two thousand years ago, and now we are commanded to bear our cross in these last days. The cross is a symbol of the affliction, persecution, and suffering Christ Jesus endured so that we might live forever with Him in eternity. While it is human nature to avoid pain and affliction, both are necessary to build up our perseverance and patience so that we might one day become complete, needing nothing (James 1:3-4). Pain and suffering are essential because the Bible says a person who suffers in his flesh has ceased sinning, seeking to do God's will and not his own (1 Peter 4:1). Many Christians are confused about what carrying their cross means today. Bearing your cross means dying to your flesh nature and living according to the commands of Christ Jesus through the power of His Holy Spirit. Today, some in the church say, "If we are saved by grace and not works, what does it matter anyway?" The answer is genuine belief in Christ Jesus produces good results because our new life reflects our Lord and Savior's life who died for us. The Bible says if we intentionally sin after we receive the knowledge of the truth, there remains no more sacrifice for sins (Hebrews 10:26). Professed believers who have not had a change of heart and still practice those same Gentiles' ways are fearful of judgment and fiery indignation that is the reward of the wicked. Gentiles hiding behind their cross are people who profess to be reborn into the Kingdom of God by water and The Spirit but continue to practice these types of things publicly or secretly: anger, wrath, fornication, uncleanliness, inordinate affection, covetous, malice, blasphemy, and filthy communication. These sins and others like them are examples of our flesh nature that we must deny and place on our cross. Issues plaguing current Gentiles hiding behind their crosses today are the belief that it's only a matter of what you say and do, even if you have not dealt with your heart problems. Your true discipleship consists of 1.) accountability to God the creator as the only standard of truth, knowledge, wisdom, and understanding. Any knowledge in this world that opposes the knowledge of God must be definitively rejected. There is no compromise. 2.) your responsibility to be obedient to Christ Jesus as Lord and Savior who died for you. The Bible says this is your reasonable service. This accountability to God and responsibility to Christ Jesus cements and bears witness of who you are, meaning your likeness (character) and image (function, behavior).

The Bible says God knows who is His are and let everyone who names the name of the Lord depart from iniquity (2 Timothy 2:19). This command is complex for some to grasp because our obsession with appearances and what things feel like complicate our already limited understanding of the spiritual will God desires versus the natural will of man that so easily deceives us. There are characteristics of God's children that make them stand out from the rest of society like a sore thumb. We contain His Holy Spirit that acts as our conscious:

- Advising us of judgment
- Warning us of sin
- Reminding us of the righteousness in Christ Jesus, who sits at the Father's right hand and intercedes for us

Another feature that stands out is their ability to continue to love not just those who love us back but all people, neighbors, enemies, and the brethren created in the image and likeness of God. The command to love for God's children means doing no harm to anyone but being faithful to others by sharing the truth (Romans 10:13). This incredible attribute comes directly from the Father, and it is a telltale sign that a person remains positioned in Christ Jesus through the power of the Holy Spirit.

Despite the Lord, our God telling His children, "My ways are not your ways and my thoughts, not your thoughts," we still seek humankind's limited wisdom (Isaiah 55:8-9).

The children of the promise still leaned on their limited understanding. They did everything they promised Him they would not do and kept ignoring and rejecting His offer to be His special called-out people.

Even with this extraordinary grace that covered our sins and saved us from eternal damnation, there was a problem, as there always is, concerning commitment and consistency for fallen humankind. The issue is not all Gentiles who profess salvation have fully understood or complied with the conditions for redemption. For some, salvation sounds good, and they want it, but not the process of sacrifice, denying oneself, and sanctification associated with becoming a "True

Believer." Many still need to fully complete their regeneration and transformation process, as the Apostle Paul, who Christ Jesus designated as the minister to the Gentiles, alluded to in his letters.

Apostle Paul described six characteristics of Gentiles (Ephesians 2:1-5) as "formerly" having given up these ways to be now living in Christ Jesus:

- Dead in your transgressions and sins
- Followed the ways of this world and its father
- Gratifying cravings of our sinful nature
- Following selfish desires and thoughts
- Objects of wrath before God
- No hope

Gentiles "hiding behind a cross" proclaim to be saved but still operate in the ways outlined above and live in the delusion that God, somehow in Christ Jesus, will accept them anyway. These Gentiles hiding behind the cross that Jesus gave His sinless life for so that they may be free have built an imaginary Jesus that best suits how they want to live. These Gentiles wish to follow their desires regardless of whether it aligns with the values and teachings of the living Jesus of the Holy Bible.

Several floating pieces are at work here, making it extremely difficult to make disciples of all nations as commanded in this current age. Four of the deep-receded problem areas that enable the Gentiles behind a Cross syndrome are as follows:

- The apostasy
- The misunderstanding of the truth
- The hardness of people's hearts toward anything uncomfortable
- The false teachings of some past and present pastors, preachers, apostles, and evangelists.

Of such teachings, for example, is one of the most deceitful misappropriated scripture references "We are saved by grace, not by works!" The capstone statement of this New Age New Testament Church, this teaching puts to death the law given by God to Moses, and the statement Christ Jesus emphatically denied letting the Jews and the world know that he had come not to abolish the law but to fulfill it (Matthew 5:17). Despite numerous verses stating we are created for good works (Ephesians 2:10), you will be judged by your works (Revelation 2:19) or this transformative realization that you will live and not die because of your works, (John 5: 28-29). It might be a good idea to unpack what "works" means biblically. Christ Jesus told us that people do not hear because they do not belong to God (John 8:47).

Good works established through New Covenant were instituted in and through our Lord and Savior Christ Jesus by the power of the Holy Spirit (Ephesians 2:10). We have mentioned that the enemy uses anything and everything of God in a perverted way to steal, kill, and destroy (John 10:10). We also know that the enemy gets a lot of help from his friend called the flesh, or our earthly will and desires. Confusion, drama, and denial happened over time when teachers and preachers failed to properly differentiate between works associated with obeying the law that will not save you (Galatians 3:1) and **works of the Holy Spirit in all True Believers. Any works or righteousness that is not a direct result of faith in the blood of Christ Jesus is not acceptable to God (John 14:6). The Old Covenant was based on a person's obedience to the written law of God; however, the works of the Holy Spirit that produce character and image regeneration are written in the hearts of the children of God.**

The Third Expose: All these things the Gentiles seek

Worrying about clothes, eating, and drinking should not be the practice of born-again Christians, though many of us, including myself, sometimes revert to these things. The difference as true Christ-followers is that we repent of these ways because we know it is wrong to depend on and worship anything other than God in Christ Jesus. Repenting means you can't continue to operate in that line of attitude, thinking, and the subsequent behavior that stems from the previous two actions. True repentance is more than just what you say.

God will always gauge what you say by your fruit. Jesus didn't say that you will know a person by what they do; Jesus said you would know a person by their fruit. *Fruit* is a product of not only what you do. Fruit is a product of why you do it and, just as importantly, what you do, and when having the opportunity to do something selfish, you resist the temptation.

The Fourth Expose: Government

The current government system and its leaders promote oppressing, controlling, and jailing the poor while encouraging and supporting their wealthy counterparts. The poor and oppressed have always had a knee on their neck, suffocating them of justice and mercy. There is no support or compassion for the fatherless, widow, or mentally and physically handicapped. Those who blaspheme the Holy Spirit, calling things abominable in the sight of God acceptable like divorce, homosexuality, fornication, and all the secret sins man hides in his wicked heart operate as if there is no judgment approaching.

People who flip the Word of God around to accomplish their own will are acting in deception and futility because God knows our hearts and motives. Once we have asked and then received The Holy Spirit, the Bible says we should not grieve Him or fight against the work He is trying to accomplish in our daily lives. The Kingdom of God will never dwell in Gentiles because they live unacceptable ways before the Lord, neither seeing Him nor knowing Him (John 14:17).

True Believers rely only on what God has written in the Holy Scriptures and on our hearts through the indwelling of the Holy Spirit (2 Timothy 3:16-17, Jeremiah 31:33). My opinions or anyone else's views amount to a hill of beans. A thing is only valid to a True Believer if Christ Jesus, by the power of the Holy Spirit, said it. We believe this because this is what Jesus says about this subject. After all, only He knows all things (John 16:30). The Bible says outside are the dogs, those who practice magic arts, the sexually immoral, the murderers, the idolaters, and everyone who loves and practices falsehood (Revelation 22:15). These are the Gentiles hiding behind a cross because they cannot enter the Kingdom of God (1 Corinthians 6:10) and are disqualified from participation in the Kingdom of Heaven (Matthew 5:20).

The Fifth Expose: Search the Heart and Test the Mind

Gentiles hiding behind a cross believe in the futility of their minds that God in Christ Jesus and the power of the Holy Spirit can be compromised with or mocked (Galatians 6:7).

They continue to operate under this crude assumption simply because of the delusion of time they have been afforded through grace. Somehow, they fake it through life, pretending to love, care for, and respect others, but they only care about themselves in their hearts. These Gentiles periodically and strategically perform gestures of superficial kindness, seeking to make it into the Kingdom undetected and under pretenses. They don't realize that our Lord and Savior has been authorized and will roll the tape on everybody who has ever lived, meaning there will be a life review of what you have done in your body in your time here in your EARTH suit. The Bible says as simply and plainly as this, "a time is coming when all who is in the graves will hear His voice, and come out, those who have done good things, to the resurrection of life and those who have done wicked things to the resurrection of condemnation," (John 5:28-29).

Gentiles hiding behind a cross are not the same as saints who fell yet are carrying their cross. The difference between saints who mess up because of the challenges of this life into brief periods or instances of sin is that they don't stay or live there as if it doesn't matter. They also repent by demonstrating accountability for what they have done wrong through the conviction of the Holy Spirit that sanctifies all True Believers.

Many things defile us; the lusts of the hearts, the dishonoring of the bodies, homosexuality, unrighteousness, unforgiveness, wickedness, covetous, maliciousness, full of envy and murder, debate, deceit, malignity, whisperers, backbiters, haters of God, spiteful, proud, boasters, inventors of evil things, disobedient to parents, without understanding, covenant breakers, without natural affection, implacable, unmerciful and taking pride and pleasure in not only doing these things but enticing others to do the same (Romans 1:29-32).

The Seventh Expose: Signs, Symptoms, and Mental State Test yourself, or you could be a Gentile hiding behind a cross that cannot and will not save you on the day of Christ Jesus! You can't build your cross. Jesus has already paid the price in blood for your salvation. You must die to this world, your will, and serve Christ Jesus with your life, heart, mind, body, soul, and all your strength. Gentiles hiding behind a cross have severe allergic reactions to the word "works." It is used some 800 times or more in the Bible, but people of this church age are anemic to anything that sounds of accountability when it comes to the Bible. Not being accountable to authority is unfortunate in any facet of life in these EARTH suits, but even more, concerning your eternal well-being. Nevertheless, salvation has come to the Gentiles, just as God has commanded (Isaiah 49:5-6) and echoed in the teaching of Paul in (Romans 11:11). The Bible says you must bear your cross and don't start until you can bear the costs (Luke 14:27).

The Holy Scriptures say, "And He shall show judgment to the Gentiles" (Matthew 12:18). Help has been sent in the Son Christ Jesus so that the Gentiles hiding behind their cross can live and not die. Some attitudes and behaviors you might want to pay attention to are partialities, hating your brother, promoting the separation between God and government to condone immoral behavior, and all forms of heart disease.

Why are all these important? There is a cutoff point, and judgment will commence. We are fast approaching that day and possibly on the cuffs of its fruition. The Bible says that when the whole number of Gentiles has been accounted for, Israel's blindness will be lifted, and the Jews will be saved (Romans 11:25). As we stated before, all these things we are going through will not get any better if you are a part of this world (2 Timothy 3:13). As True Believers, we say and try to live, for the most part, the statement, "We are in the world but not of the world." The age of the church will not last very long at all. The Lord has stated, "I come back quickly," (Revelation 22:20). The time is quickly upon us, and this world is literally on life support. The plug is about to be pulled. The Bible says, "I have sent my angel to give you this testimony for the churches; I am the Root and the Offspring of David, the Bright and Morning Star, The Spirit, the bride, and him whomsoever hears say come!" (Revelation 22:16-17).

Envision the Promise: He redeemed us so that the blessing given to Abraham might come to the Gentiles through Christ Jesus so that by faith, we might receive the promise of the Spirit (Galatians 3:14). But we should always give thanks to God for you, brethren beloved by the Lord, because God has chosen you from the beginning for salvation through sanctification by the Spirit and faith in the Truth (2 Thessalonians 2:13).

Chapter Eight
PEANUT BUTTER AND JELLY

"Jesus answered them and said, Verily, verily, I say unto you, Ye seek me, not because ye saw the miracles, but because ye did eat of the loaves, and were filled, (John 6:26). 'For the bread of God is He who comes down from heaven and gives life to the world," (John 6:33). 'Then the Lord said to Moses, "Behold, I will rain bread from heaven for you. And the people shall go out and gather a certain quota every day, that I may test them, whether they will walk in My law or not," (Exodus 16:4). 'For the grace of God that brings salvation has appeared to all men, teaching us that, denying ungodliness and worldly lusts, we should live soberly, righteously, and godly in the present age," (Titus 2:11-12).

The First Expose: PB & J

The Peanut Butter and Jelly sandwich is primarily an American comfort food delicacy that young children and old have enjoyed since the early 1900s. The PB & J sandwich has three ingredients consisting of four items. These ingredients include two slices of bread, peanut butter, and jelly. When combined with correct ratios, these four items produce a delectable meal enjoyed by people worldwide in the last half of this century. I propose metaphorically and by comparison that the simple peanut butter and jelly sandwich illustrates the condition and position of some 21st Century Christians in today's society. The ingredients and the structure give a complete picture of the current Christian mindset toward grace and holiness. Just as Americans have a tradition of eating peanut butter and jelly sandwiches, Christians also possess a tradition of rebellion and disobedience to the known will of God to do their will. This self-will often comes at the expense of misplaced religious and government-related ordinances, statutes, and legality. In comparison, many confess to being children of God's Kingdom for convenience. They often hide behind religious and governmental rules and regulations to avoid doing the will of God and control others around them.

The Second Expose: The True Bread

There is no controversy among believers and unbelievers alike that food and water are essential to sustain human life. Yet, our Lord and Savior explained that man could not live by just food and water alone, but only the True Bread from heaven (Matthew 4:4). What does that mean? There is life after this mortal life, and this earthly bread, the food we eat necessary to sustain this body, does not suffice in the next life. Upon the expiration of our E³ART³H suit, all will enter immediately to a spiritual place, which requires spiritual sustenance. The Holy Scriptures are clear that flesh and blood will not inherit the Kingdom of God (1 Corinthians 15:50). The first ingredient is the top slice of bread of the PB&J sandwich representing the True Bread from heaven, Christ Jesus. The bread He refers to is His body that would later be sacrificed holy, blameless, and sinless so that we might live forever in eternity with Him. This True Bread, which took away all the sins of all humanity, is the only acceptable way for anyone to inherit eternal life (John 14:6). The True Bread replaced the law given by Moses, supplying every need of man both naturally and spiritually. If you understand you will live and not die, you can understand what Jesus means by "I am the true Bread of Life." The problem humankind has in his soul is not that he will die, the real problem is that he will live. Jesus tells the people of His day, just as His word tells us today, the truth about what happens when someone completes this life in this E³ART³H suit. According to your work done in this earthly body, you will live somewhere in eternity. The good raised to a resurrection of life eternal, and the evil was raised as well but to an eternity of condemnation in the lake of fire (Revelation 20:15). The True Bread is the Word of God in the flesh, the propitiation for the sins of the whole world.

The Third Expose: Grace Holds It Together

The grace of God in Christ Jesus is the peanut butter, the second and essential ingredient that holds the other three components together. Peanut butter depicts the grace of God manifested itself spiritually, empowering humankind with the opportunity to serve Christ Jesus and attain eternal life. Physically grace is the embodiment of Christ Jesus sent from heaven as the means of our salvation. Grace through faith is the foundation of the New Testament covenant, in which the penalty of all sins, which is death, is forgiven by belief in Christ Jesus. Grace isn't a work of humanity for doing something good; grace is the gift of God given freely to demonstrate His goodness and faithfulness toward humankind. However, for the PB&J Christian, the grace of God in Christ Jesus is perverted to practice ungodliness and worldly lusts despite its purpose to live soberly, righteously, and godly in these last days (Titus 2:12-13). Just as Americans have a tradition of eating peanut butter and jelly sandwiches, Christians also practice a tradition of rebellion and disobedience to the known will of God to accomplish their plans and not His will for their lives. This behavior often comes through the vehicle of misplaced and oppressive religious and government-related ordinances, statutes, and legality. In comparison, PB&J Christians confess to being children of God's Kingdom for convenience. They often hide behind artificial religious doctrines and unjust governmental rules and regulations to avoid God's will and hypocritically control others around them.

The Fourth Expose: The Word Is Sweet.

Jelly, the third ingredient of the PB&J sandwich, is the Word of God. The Word of God is His inspired written instruction for us in godliness and righteousness while we remain in this E³ART³H suit (2 Timothy 3:16). Every Word of God is tested and true; it is life for those who take refuge in it and a sword that cuts through Spirit and soul. Everything in this world will perish, but the Word of God will live forever (Isaiah 40:8). The Word of God is pure, uncompromised, and consistent from the beginning of Genesis 1:1 to the end of Revelation 22:21.

The Fifth Expose: Perishable Bread

The fourth and final ingredient in the PB&J sandwich is the bottom slice of bread, representing humanity's earthly, flesh laden will that naturally opposes the will of God due to its sinful nature. Our bread rationalizes the primary job of The True Bread, grace, and the Word of God is to do whatever we bid to satisfy our carnal wants and desires as long as we believe and ask Him in faith. Of course, this is not how the Kingdom of God works, but people do believe and live

179

according to this false doctrine in these last days. Though they may have the principle of faith, PB&J Christians have omitted the doctrine of the Lord and Savior. Many live in ignorance or denial and have not transitioned with Jesus, as discussed in Chapter Four, from His first assignment as the Lamb of God, who takes away the world's sins through His death, crucifixion, and burial (John 1:29). That wasn't the end of the story because three days later, He arose to where He is this day sitting at the Father's right hand in heaven (Hebrews 1:3). The Lord's next assignment is when He returns, just like He said He would and will be gathering up His Church in preparation for His glorious day. This day is called The Day of Christ, where the long arm of our Lord and Savior will gather His Church unto Himself in avoidance of the great tribulation or the time of God's wrath on the earth. The will of man claims in pretense and appearance to align with the True Bread but, in his heart, is far from it. The heart of man also perverts the Word of God, misrepresenting, misquoting, incorrectly discerning, and applying the Word of God in their lives and teaching others. For the PB&J sandwich Christian, this is not blatant often, but the secret sins of the heart are carried out through religious and governmental persecution of the poor and oppressed in this present age. In this age of racism, religious oppression, lawlessness, technological arrogance, irresponsibility, and manslaughter, it is apparent that the fulfillment of the Gentiles has all but reached its plateau.

The Sixth Expose: Misplaced Religiosity

Rebellion and disobedience to God are nothing new to God. Before the beginning of time, God dealt with rebellion, starting with the devil and one-third of the angels with him, banishing them to outer darkness, the preformed earth. God's first man, Adam, and his bride, Eve, His chosen people, His priests, prophets, humanity, and now His church to this very day, have grieved God's soul with their wicked hearts. The Bible says every inclination of a man's heart is always evil (Genesis 6:5). When humanity does not want to do the will of God, they have always used religion and government to justify themselves in their own eyes and for others to validate their blatant disobedience and rebellion to the known will of God. The Bible says every way of a man is right in his own eyes, but the Lord weighs the heart (Proverbs 21:2). God's people used religion to thwart His divine will for them throughout history when they were experiencing success for any period of time without his direct hand upon them. They tended to veer off into idol worship and develop a heart for worldly things, which often were the very things the good Lord was trying to save them from experiencing.

There have been three eras of God's children, beginning with the original children of the promise and ending here in the age of the church and all found a way to attempt life on their own. All share unique experiences that separate them from each other and other groups globally, yet the profession of these three groups has remained the same. The existence of God has never been the issue with these people, yet unity and consistency to date are unachieved. Though existing in different times, with superior technological advances, and a great set of witnesses to God's grace, mercy, and goodness, their hearts remained unchanged. These attributes of God's children are as follows:

The Manna Kids: the original children of the promise, saw the hand of God literally on several occasions. They experienced the miracles in Egypt, walked across the Red Sea on dry land while watching their enemies behind them drown, but continually displayed these unacceptable attributes: murmured, never satisfied, rebellious, disobeyed God, faithless, continued with a slave mentality although they were free, built idols; ignored commands, decrees, statutes, laws, ordinances, and precepts, hard hearts, motives, intentions, and opportunities were wicked, evil, and embodied selfish always.

The Fish Sandwich Kids: These individuals were the chosen generation who would live to see and touch the prophesied Messiah. The Holy Scriptures say many people longed to see His coming, an opportunity that The Fish Sandwich Kids foolishly dismissed.

- Witnessed Christ Jesus in the flesh

- Murmured, never satisfied

- Did not know God

- Did not believe God

- Refused to repent

- Did not recognize the Son of God or Son of Man

- Operated on a Piece of Jesus Mentality

- Rejected signs, miracles, and wonders because of spiritual blindness and had hard hearts.

PB&J Christians: Fully completed Bible, access to the Holy Spirit, the most technologically advanced in all creation. But like or worse than the generations before them, they choose to:

- Deny the work of the Holy Spirit, sanctification

- Claim Jesus but have attributes and ways of the devil

- Misuse grace to avoid doing the will of God

- Take the Word of God out of context to justify disobedience and rebellion

- Conveniently accomplish their will while negating the will of our Lord and Savior Christ Jesus

- Deny truth

- The hardness of their hearts

- No ability to effectively witness to this lost world

- Worship Jesus in pretense with their mouths, not their hearts.

The Lord knew this about humans and His people. What has always happened with humankind is that, despite knowing the Lord, believers habitually grow impatient and restless with what they can't immediately naturally touch, visually see, or feel in their Spirit in a gratifying, controlling, or self-preserving manner. This condition is why in the beginning, He placed a host of different types of laws, commands, statutes, commemorative feasts, and festivals consistently happening each year to ensure that the people remembered their covenant with Him. An old cliche says, "out of sight, out of mind," meaning what we don't see regularly, we don't retain. This saying is priceless when associated with God's people and their adulterous relationship with Him. However, the New Covenant has positioned accountability to God and responsibility to Christ Jesus squarely in the professed Christian's ability to believe in the Son of God and Man alone.

The Seventh Expose: Hiding Behind Democracy

In the Kingdom of Heaven to come, there is no governmental entity known as democracy, no voting, dictatorship, or any other form of government besides Jesus Christ as Lord, Savior, and King. This form of government is a problem, especially for the USA. You only need to look at the history of the fruit of this country to know it suffers from chronic heart disease. If the Kingdom of God or Heaven was a democracy, anyone who doesn't accept Jesus as King and ruler of heaven and the earth only needs to find another place to call home after the expiration of their E³ART³H suit. That's it. However, this human intellectual reasoning poses a significant problem.

The flip side of that statement depicted here is what the Bible says. **"Then I saw a great White Throne and Him who sat on it, from whose face the earth and the heaven fled. And there was no place for them,"** *(Revelation 20:11)*. Guess who "*them*" is? Either you are a part of His church in the

Kingdom of God, or you are a Gentile whose reward is only the lake of fire and brimstone (Revelation 20:15). There is no in-between, even if you are a confused Gentile hiding behind the cross. That doesn't mean True Believers should ignore democracy or any other established form of government. The point is government should not be idolized or abused like everything else connected to the Christians' walk. We live in this world as True Believers. Still, we were chosen out of it by our Lord and Savior Christ Jesus for eternal life with Him (John 15:19). PB&J Christians have twisted, ignored, rebelled against, and disobeyed God's holy mandate for His people who love Him and are called according to His divine purpose to love one another and treat others as they want to be treated (John 14:21). PB&J Christians misuse the government legislature's legal power and authority by manipulating and controlling people and resources. They have worshipped other false gods all to the eventual arousal of the anger of God (despite His patience) against them, repenting not until after suffering or being threatened with dire consequences. God's children separate from what they know to what they feel, think, and frequently rationalize in the futility of their minds. The heart of man, which contains his imaginations, thoughts, and behaviors, is uncontrollable unless brought under submission to God and the obedience of Christ Jesus. Where have we gone wrong in the church doctrine that has gotten us this far off track? For humanity to realize the necessity and need of God in his life, God first chose a group of people whom He would call His special possession out of all the different groups of people he had created on the earth. This group of people called the Jews, provided that they were obedient to God and followed His commands, decrees, precepts, statutes, and laws, would have providential treatment compared to all other groups because of their relationship with the Lord our God. Because of their C4 condition and D5 predisposition, they could only sometimes keep their side of the covenant or agreement they had made to the Lord. Instead of receiving all the blessings that came with obedience to the Lord, they got the flip side curses because of rebellion, disobedience, and rejection of God's will for their own.

The Eighth Expose: The Nothing New Under the Sun

Peanut Butter and Jelly Sandwich Christians are not new, but merely a changed appearance of God's people in Christ Jesus throughout the generations. The hearts are the same, and the appearance of godliness is the same, so the lack of true power in the Holy Spirit remains the same. They've always been here, doing what they always do, which is rejecting the truth because of the same three things. They don't know the Lord and His ways, don't believe the Lord, and refuse to repent of their ways that are unacceptable to the holiness of God. The sad news is that some will still refuse to repent of their evil ways in these last days, even upon our Lord's return (Revelation 9:21).

A broad pathway leads an afflicted individual down the road of error, deception, rebellion, disobedience, and disbelief. Still, there is a narrow and straight road that leads to life. As corrupt as this generation is today, it is hard to fathom that this road to destruction didn't end here with us with all the technology, brilliance, and so-called genius people in the twenty-first century claim to have. The Book of Knowledge says there is nothing new under the sun for humankind, for what has been done again will be repeated, so seemingly, we should be able to avoid past mistakes. However, understanding man's predisposition to prevent bad choices will never work in man's favor because of his control issues. Much wisdom brings much grief, and increased knowledge brings increased sorrow (Ecclesiastes 1:18). We know this to be true because we have a book with detailed and accurate documentation that depicts very candidly and transparently the end of this story (Revelation 1:19). We have followed that pathway to produce its final natural and unprofitable fruit, The Peanut Butter and Jelly Sandwich Christian.

Envision the Promise: But this shall be the covenant that I will make with the House of Israel. "After those days, saith the Lord, I will put my law in their inward parts, and write it in their hearts; and I will be their God, and they shall be my people," (Jeremiah 31:33).

Chapter Nine
TIS' THE SEASON (TIME IS SHORT)

"Watch ye, therefore, and pray always, that ye may be accounted worthy to escape all these things that shall come to pass, and to stand before the Son of man," (Luke 21:36); "Blessed are those servants whom the master when he comes, will find watching. Assuredly, I say to you that he will gird himself and have them sit down to eat and will come and serve them. And if he should come in the second watch, or come in the third watch, and find them so, blessed are those servants," (Luke 12:37-38). "For the Lord, Himself will descend from heaven with a shout, with the voice of an archangel, and with the trumpet of God. And the dead in Christ will rise first. Then we who are alive and remain shall be caught up together with them in the clouds to meet the Lord in the air. And thus, we shall always be with the Lord," (I Thessalonians 4:16-17).

The First Expose: (TIS) Time is Short

The Christmas song ushering in the holiday season entitled

"Tis the Season" is known worldwide as an indicator that Christmas and New Year's holidays are fast approaching. As it is in the natural, so it is in the spiritual, by the signs in the heavens and the earth, some can speculate that the end times, as prophesied in the Holy Scriptures, are upon this generation (McClure). The Bible says, 'Therefore, rejoice, O heavens, and you who dwell in them! Woe to the inhabitants of the earth and the sea! The devil has come down to you, having great wrath, because he knows that he has a short time," (Revelation 12:12). These times that have come to fruition should make any unbeliever second guess their theology in disputing a Righteous, Supreme, and Holy God in Christ Jesus. Righteous because His word confirms that these evil days will come, and He will return to judge every man for his deeds. Supreme being, there is nothing you, I, or anyone besides God Himself can do to change our condition eternally or internally. Holy affirms God's character, justice, and faithfulness in His will for His people and the inhabitants of this earth. Many people foolishly play Russian roulette with their eternity; some will continue in their sinful ways right up until Jesus comes back to retrieve His Church. This writing is intended for the reader not to fail an open book test but rather to repent and prepare for what's ahead. Historically, humanity has not introduced any plausible explanation for creating something from nothing! The best that the science of this world can do is to make from what already exists. No scientist to date has ever created anything. God, the Creator of this universe, planet, earth, and everything in it is the only Living Being capable of creation. No philosopher has ever come close to disproving the intelligent design of a Supreme, All-powerful, All-knowing, and Living God. This world has a rapidly debilitating problem recognizing that time is short, and the clock is ticking. Time has a beginning and an end; eternity does not. Humankind doesn't understand eternal things, and because of this, he denies it in his heart. The blatant pride of this world that increases with every invention and discovery increases humankind's defiance of the written will of God and leads it down a rabbit hole in which many will not return.

The Second Expose: The Timeline of the 21st-Century Church

Because of the times we are in, there are many things the existing churches, congregations, and leadership need to focus on to prepare the hearts of the people for the coming of the Lord. First, as long as we keep referring to the building as the church and never consider that, ultimately, the "church" is inside each individual, we will never achieve the one mind necessary to fight these spiritual battles that have engulfed this world. So many unacceptable doctrines and heresies have become commonplace in the house of the Lord. The Bible commands us in this day to "'Come out from among them and be separate," says the Lord. 'Do not touch what is unclean, and I will receive you,'" (2 Corinthians 6:17). Yes, we are to assimilate, encourage, and exhort one another, but not at the expense of defiling ourselves or neglecting our responsibility of bearing our own cross every day as our Savior commanded (Luke 9:23). This chapter presents a visual timeline of past events, current events, and the known events documented in the Bible so that believers can better comprehend how much of these events have been and are taking place as I write tonight. I have been following one pastor out of Milton, Florida, Pastor Robert Breaker, who uses a visual timeline every time he preaches. One timeline Pastor Breaker drew was very detailed and gave some of the different hypotheses or versions of what the gathering of the church might look like and all the events leading up and unto that glorious day when our Lord and Savior is revealed for all the world to acknowledge and behold.

The Rapture of the Church

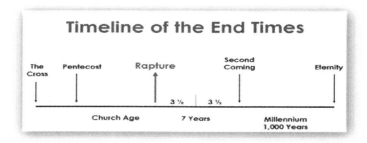

LAW CHRIST CHURCH AGE RAPTURE???

TRIBULATION MILLENNIUM ——————-|----------

----|---------------|----------------------|------- --------——|-------------

------------- (Johns)

Grace Begins Grace End Here Testing of Nations 1000 Year Reign

You are "HERE," and we are almost "THERE."

The Book of Wisdom tells us to watch and observe what is happening around us, or we will get caught sleeping if we fail to acknowledge and heed the warning signs mentioned above for the gathering of the True Church by our Lord and Savior. Pay careful attention then, redeeming the time because the days are evil, walking not as unwise but as wise (Ephesians 5:16). The entirety of all we have covered thus far is summed up in this one verse before mentioned. Everything we have talked about is to give you the biblical perspective of the truth of what has happened, what is happening, and according to the Word of God, which is the most reliable document on earth, of what is destined to occur in a very short time from now (Bible IQ). Please read your Bibles! Ask the Lord God of Hosts to open your spiritual eyes and ears to what His messengers are saying to "the churches" (Revelation 3:6) so that you will become a part of the "True Church." This church is the Lord's enduring Church and the one He promised to return and retrieve (Luke 21:36). There is a point and a set time when the anger of the Lord will not be restrained, and He will proceed to do what He said He would do (Revelation 6:17). The Bible says but they mocked the messengers of God, despising His words and misusing His prophets until the wrath of the Lord rose against them until there was no remedy (2 Chronicles 36:16).

The Third Expose: Spiritual Warfare

Days of Noah Part II The Reign of Fire. I've said throughout this book, "People don't believe God is who He says He is and that He is going to do to the letter what He says He is going to do. There's no more transparent picture of this truth than the depiction of the Days of Noah when God sent the rain to destroy humankind because of the evilness of his heart (Genesis 6:17). After repeated warnings for one hundred and twenty years, time ran out for man as a result of the works of their own hands, their self-sabotage nature, and their refusal to repent (Genesis 6:3). God selected one righteous man named Noah and his seven family members to continue humankind. God did what He said, destroyed every living thing on earth, and created a covenant with Noah and all living flesh. The covenant stated He would never again destroy all flesh by flood and marked it the heavens by the sign of the rainbow (Genesis 9:15-16).

Many have ignored the signs, and this generation has far exceeded the wickedness any nation in the previous generations could have dreamed of due to increased technology. In this season, these times are appropriately called the Days of Noah Part II: The Reign of Fire, mentioned by many prophets and our Lord and Savior Christ Jesus describing the last days. Judgment spiritually referred to as *fire*, is the verdict for all humanity, everything under heaven, Hades, the grave, and in the sea, beginning with the church by our Lord and Savior. Each person's work in his EARTH suit will undergo a heart and mind inspection to determine his final home. His home is one of two places, acceptable with Christ Jesus wherever He is or the place of fire and brimstone. This warning is why we must pay careful attention now, redeeming the time because the days are evil, living our lives knowing that imminent judgment is close (Ephesians 5:16). All we have covered are efforts to do our part in warning all who will hear that a shaking of all things is coming (Haggai 2:8). The Apostle Peter said, "But the end of all things is at hand: therefore, be serious and watchful in your prayers," (1 Peter 4:7). Very few people understand the totality of all that is happening these last days. The disbelief that Satan exists and is actively leading this current world's affairs, coupled with the ignorance of the spiritual wars for our souls, is too much for this generation to conceive. So, in their human wisdom, they deny the Bible, depending on their limited understanding, and call everything a conspiracy theory or religious foolishness. So, just like in the Days of Noah, people continue to:

• Practice immorality

• Worship idols

• Eat and drink excessively

• Marry and give in marriage

• Disregard the warnings of the prophet

• Buy and sell

• Plant crops

• Build infrastructure

• Lack of spiritual awareness

One difference, however, is that many today are aware that the end of all things is an absolute possibility, naturally or supernaturally speaking. Some choose to ignore or deny the truth while everything crumbles around them. Nothing currently in this world gives you any hope other than the assurance that this world is on the brink of war, famine, plagues, and destruction of this earth. These current events coincide with the biblical, Kingdom-oriented perspective of current and future events. The foolish still reject the Word of God simply because it is easier not to believe. The darkness is indeed coming and is already working among us, contributing heavily to the fear, panic, uncertainty, and distrust we find in every area and facet of this life. Nothing on this side of heaven is immune, and all will experience the trials and testing of this age. The mission of the True Church is to set the example of patience and perseverance by faith and endure to the end. The lack of peace within the body of Christ is producing a plethora of anxiety-induced men, women, and children that are at best distracted but at worst delusional, meaning the hand of the Lord is against them because they like to do what is evil (2 Thessalonians 2:12-13). Just as in the Days of Noah, they mocked God's messenger, despised His words, and scoffed at his prophet until the rain came down forty days straight, flooding the entire earth, and did not recede until a hundred and fifty days (Genesis 8:3).

The Fifth Expose: Spiritual Warfare the Teachings of Balaam

The salvation and sanctification process involves spiritual growth through hearing the Word of God. Hearing and then doing the commands of the word produces character and behaviors acceptable to God through obedience to our Lord and Savior, Christ Jesus. The Holy Spirit who lives in us is our witness and promise from the Lord, sealing us for the day of redemption in Christ Jesus, who died for every True Believer. This attribute makes us Holy and separates us, the True Believer, from any other nation.

Despite how good people think they are, anyone suffering from unbelief has no defense or resistance against his sinful nature, whether from the devil, this world, or even the person themselves. In fact, we are our own worst enemy regarding submission, sacrifice, and the control issues we deal with daily in this E³ART³H suit. Further, without the Spirit, a person cannot discern between biblical church doctrine of the truth that will save one's soul, contrary to a useless, convenient gospel that is often preached today. The teaching of Balaam represents the false religious teachers and corrupt, ungodly government leaders in this present age. Like the prophet Balaam who chased money instead of God, disobeyed God, and even taught the children of the promise to worship idols, eat food sacrificed to idols and practice sexual immorality as the teachers of this age do likewise (Revelation 2:14). The character and the behaviors imitated by these Balaam teachers and teachings include:

• False prophets

• Compromised theology

• Eating food sacrificed to idols

• Sexual immorality

• Covetousness

• Idolatry

• Greed

• Love wages of unrighteousness.

The teachings of Balaam are the root cause of the new twenty-first-century apostasy. It is not a rare occasion; it is the norm to turn on the radio or TV any day or night and receive false, misinterpreted, prosperity-derived teaching. Regardless of religious denomination, there has yet to be a consensus on who, what, or why all these things have come about. The causes of the dire situation that this world is currently in are subjective, but the fact is we are here now. You might ask where "here" is. That is an excellent question because "here" is this point in history that is a time of reckoning and coming to terms with what you truly believe about the end of this world as we know it. It has just been proved right before your eyes and mine that even in this day of technological genius, this world can succumb to a life-altering, world-ending event. While natural and manufactured catastrophes are happening at unprecedented and astronomical rates compared to other times in history, it goes unmentioned in the mainstream media for useless and stacked information that swells and manipulates people's pleasures, offenses, and emotions. So, the time is here in all of our lives where denial is not an option, and we need to be clear about what we believe and why we believe it because our very eternity is dependent upon it. Most people think living in denial and ignorance is safer, which has never been a good option. Not confronting your fears or issues has never successfully made any afflicted person's grey hairs and problems disappear. My assignment is to write what I see so that people don't play Russian roulette with their eternity. Anyone choosing not to fail the open book test that leads to eternal life has an opportunity.

The Sixth Expose: Spiritual Warfare Sodom and Gomorrah

The third spiritual war operating as we speak and running rampant throughout the world is the immorality of sex, idol worship, and wickedness. The biblical cities of Sodom and

Gomorrah are where examples were made for sins so grave it had come to the attention of the Lord for judgment (Genesis 18:20). There are very few ideologies more detrimental to this world and the church than the deception that God has somehow changed His mind about His total disgust for immoral sexual conduct (Jude 1:7). Yet, humanity and some deceived professed believers have built themselves a god and Jesus where this type of lifestyle depicts the love of their god. So, we have coined this age as Sodom and Gomorrah, the Next Chapter. Many choose to ignore or repent despite numerous scripture passages from Genesis to Revelation that this lifestyle is non-negotiable and there have been over two thousand years to get it right. This ideology would be correct because the god and Jesus they worship are not the One True God in Christ Jesus, the God of Abraham, Isaac, and Jacob. These individuals know this activity is wrong in their hearts; their flesh did not affect their reading, only their understanding of the consequences of rejecting God's laws, not believing God, and unrepentance. The trademarks of the Sodom and Gomorrah ideology include:

• Sexual immorality

• Impurity

• Unnatural sexual acts

• Fornication

- Adultery

- Perversion

- Spiritual wickedness.

The Seventh Expose: Better Days: The Flip Side

The trials and tribulations that will come upon the whole world do not have to happen to you! The Holy Scriptures says that the Lord always provides a way of escape for the godly and righteous (2 Peter 2:9). The flip side is the immediate future is not bright for the inhabitants of this present earth for those who imagine returning to the normalcy of this age. This deranged normalcy is the root of the entire problem! Nothing is usual about the times now or days ahead, except it should be a wake-up call for every living creature. Getting a jab in the arm will not fix your heart, so it is not the fix-it-all solution many want it to be, and pre-2020 normalcy won't be coming back any time soon, quite possibly ever. For those who believe the Word of God and see the times we are in, it is one of the most exciting times. The testimony of Christ Jesus is the spirit of prophecy, allowing His servants to prepare for what is in front of us as True Believers as far as the Word of God is concerned (Revelation 19:10).

In the weekly YouTube commentary "The Two Preachers," viewers can see firsthand biblical prophecy unfolding. Biweekly updates show worldwide natural catastrophes, including earthquakes, flooding, volcano eruptions, mudslides, sinkholes, severe inclement weather, forest fires, pandemics, and many other cataclysmic events, too widespread and numerous to mention them all (Birkbeck). Jesus confirmed this heaven, and this earth would pass away, but His word will not pass away. Jesus predicted these events two thousand years ago, stating that these things must happen and commanded us not to be afraid when it does. These prophesied events include wars, nation against nation, Kingdom against Kingdom, famines, droughts, pestilences, signs in the sun, moon, stars, sea, and waves roaring, and distress worldwide (Luke 21:8-11). Yet only a few people know what is happening in the next state, much less another country these days.

Envision the Promise "Because you have kept My command to persevere, I also will keep you from the hour of trial which shall come upon the whole world, to test those who dwell on the earth." "Behold, I am coming quickly! Hold fast to what you have, that no one may take your crown. He who overcomes, I will make him a pillar in the temple of My God, and he shall go out no more. I will write on him the name of My God and the name of the city of My God, the New Jerusalem, which comes down out of heaven from My God. And I will write on him My new name," *(Revelation 3:10–12)*. "Therefore rejoice, O heavens, and you who dwell in them! Woe to the inhabitants of the earth and the sea! The devil has come down to you, having great wrath, because he knows that he has a short time," *(Revelation 12:12)*.

Chapter Ten

IT TAKES TWO: THE LEGITIMACY OF YOUR WITNESS

"A single witness shall not rise against a man on account of any iniquity or any sin which he has committed; on the evidence of two or three witnesses, a matter shall be confirmed," (Deuteronomy 19:15 NASB) "and there are three witnesses on the earth: The Spirit, the water, and the blood; and these three agree [are in unison; their testimony coincides]," (1 John 5:8 AMP). "If I bear witness of Myself, my witness is not true. There is another who bears witness of Me, and I know that the witness which He witnesses of Me are true," (John 5:31-32). "The Spirit itself beareth witness with our spirit that we are the children of God," (Romans 8:16).

The First Expose: God's Witness

It bears repeating and is essential to understand that God is not a man but a Spirit. God is a Spirit may seem like a foregone conclusion. Still, this truth is a monumental philosophical concept that is a stumbling block to this world and even to the children of God at times. The Kingdom of God and Heaven design resembles a monarchy type of governmental rulership. A monarchy has one ruler having total authority to set, judge, and enforce laws, ordinances, statutes, and decrees. Correctly understanding the legitimacy and power of a Kingdom witness starts with understanding God is flawless. The Bible says the foolishness of God is wiser than men and the weakness of God stronger than men (1 Corinthians 1:25). Of course, ignorant and evil humankind takes this verse to mean God has some fault or flaw in Him, but He doesn't, and this is, in essence, man's problem. Humankind consistently tries to find a loophole, way around, or substitution for God's rules, commands, and laws. They trust technology, science, and the wisdom of mortal man (sometimes with the enemy's help) to deviate from the inerrant Word of God. Every word from the mouth of God is pure, proven, and intentional. He doesn't need to repeat Himself, not for His sake but ours. This inerrancy is why the witness is critical in the Kingdom of God and Heaven. God's Kingdom resembles a courtroom; any matter seeking confirmation in heaven, or the earth is validated by the faithful testimony of two or three witnesses. The witness's credibility is paramount; that being the case, God is by far the most excellent eyewitness of all the witnesses in the world and the universe. God has been here from the beginning, and He alone accounts for what no other spirit, human, place, animal, or thing can account for, called *origin. Origin* sets God apart from anything else that has ever existed. The first four words of the Bible state, "In the beginning, God." No human in all creation but our Lord and Savior Christ Jesus and the One like Him, the Holy Spirit, can account for this truth, for they are One. God has called the air, the seas, humanity, the animals, the heavens, the earth, the moon, the stars, and everything created as a testimony and witness of His eternal being. Everything in creation points back to God and God alone because of *origin*. No matter what man does, what he discovers, what he makes, what he thinks, what he can prove or disapprove, it has and always will at the end, pointing back to God because of *origin*. This truth is a problem and thorn in the foot of this world. Every self-proclaimed philosopher, scientist, medical doctor, educator, professor, or non-religious human being who does not acknowledge or believe in His existence will never live a life of peace in this world or the one to come until they somehow experience His presence. As we discussed before, we all have a date with a box, meaning that all men will die at least once, and then the judgment (Hebrews 9:27). But God in Christ Jesus adamantly proclaims in His good news message that the second death is an intentional choice everyone must choose to avoid by denying their sinful life for life eternal in His righteous body. This chapter suggests and explains that the Kingdom witness has exponential legal autonomy to decide a person's eternal destination.

The Second Expose: The Witness of Christ Jesus

Jesus has two distinct natures; 1.) Born of a woman making him one hundred percent Son of Man, and 2.) Born of a virgin conceived by the Holy Spirit. This God-breathed, Holy Spirit-induced birth qualifies Him as the Son of God. Jesus is the only person that ever lived, having two distinct natures that allow Him to be a witness in heaven and earth.

Further, His witness is faithful, and there was no sin in Him, but for our sakes, He complied with everything told to Him by the Father, even to the death. Throughout the Bible, Jesus had witnesses of His life, ministry, and death. The Old Testament prophets are His witnesses, the New Testament prophets are His witnesses, The Holy Spirit is His witness, and we, the church, are His witnesses. The Holy Scriptures say, "Behold; I have given Him for a witness to the people, a leader, and commander to the people," (Isaiah 55:4). John the Baptist was His witness. But One comes after me that will baptize with the Holy Spirit and fire (Matthew 3:11). His disciples are His witness. "You also must testify because you have been here from the beginning," (John 15:27). Jesus not only had the witness of man but the most important witness of all. God is His witness; "this is My Beloved Son in whom I am well pleased," (Matthew 3:17). The Holy Spirit is His witness, and He saw The Spirit of God descending like a dove and lighting upon Him (Matthew 3:16). The Holy Spirit who lives inside of every True Believer is His witness. "But one comes after me that will baptize with the Holy Spirit and fire," (Matthew 3:11). Jesus Christ is not coming back running for president or any other government position. He has already been crowned the King of the entire world in the line and succession of King David, just like God said it would happen (Luke 1:32-33). His Kingdom that He will rule on this earth will not be a democracy, and if you don't realize the differences now, you are in for a rude awakening when Jesus returns. In a Kingdom setting, the legitimacy of any contract, agreement, covenant, promise, or judicial proceeding is predicated and adjudicated by two or more witnesses. No one person's testimony is valid unless a credible witness ratifies it. Even God's testimony respects and adheres to the rules of witnessing Himself. When God swears by Himself, He refers to the fullness of the Godhead, God the Father, God the Son, and God the Holy Spirit. The point: Jesus said, "But I have a greater witness than that of John, for the works the Father have given me to finish, the same works that I do bear witness of Me, that the Father has sent Me," (John 5:36).

The Third Expose: The Witness of the Holy Spirit

God is His witness, the earth and all creation are His witnesses, and the Old Testament prophets are His witness. Jesus, Himself, bears witness to the Advocate and Spirit of Truth, named the Holy Spirit (John 14:26). The New Testament prophets and disciples are witnesses to the Holy Spirit. All true believers who have ever lived are witnesses to the Holy Spirit. "Unless I leave, He will not come, One like Me, The Comforter, the Spirit of truth, the power of God." The Holy Spirit is the one who convicts the world of sin, righteousness, and judgment. Do not "grieve" the Holy Spirit, the witness living inside you, and the one who testifies on your behalf. The legitimacy of your belief, faith, and sanctification in Christ Jesus as your lone Lord and Savior makes the Holy Spirit the most critical person in your list of contacts! The last person that you want to grieve, or yet make His presence of no consequence in your daily walk with the Lord, is the Holy Spirit. The Holy Spirit is your last line of defense and the believers' lifeline to salvation and eternal life. The Holy Spirit is the gift of God's promise in Christ Jesus made with His Church to comfort, counsel, convict, and eternally be with them until his imminent return.

As sure as the Holy Spirit is desperately trying to save your life, there is always the flip side, which is the existence of an unclean spirit that is desperately trying to ruin you and your life. The work of the unclean spirit concentrates on killing your joy in the Lord by injecting false claims that your faithfulness and obedience to God are vain and in futility. The unclean spirit, referring to satanic and demonic vices, then increases its efforts to kill your hope of the redemptive power of salvation through faith in Christ Jesus alone through grace. The unclean spirit would have you believe that working or keeping the law will save you, which he knows can only be obtained through faith in Christ Jesus alone, the gift from God! Constant meditation and focus on your past sins and what you might do in the future can lead you to disregard the promises of the Holy Scriptures and begin conformity to the ways of this fleeting world. But thanks be to God for the seal of the Holy Spirit that brings to remembrance the gospel of truth spoken by Christ Jesus to strengthen our faith walk. Finally, the ultimate goal of the unclean spirit is to create disbelief in the Believer unto death with an end game to destroy your soul. We have been speaking of this spiritual warfare, which is the fight for your eternal soul. Opposition and rebellion to the known will of God and the perversion of anything holy and sacred to God have been and are the unclean spirits' primary mission. The Holy Spirit, however, is your seal unto redemption. Regardless of whatever is going on around you and even sometimes happening to you, the Holy Spirit will keep you in perfect peace: because He that lives in you is greater than he that is in the world (1 John 4:4).

The Fourth Expose: Your Witness

Unfortunately, you are your worst witness regarding the authenticity and validity of your salvation and sanctification process. The human wisdom of this world accounts for a large portion of the spiritual blindness of this age. The delusional mindset that people are somehow good or are inherently good, or you can somehow get through this life alone, is suicide by disbelief. You may not realize it, especially in the current C4D5 chronic affliction state that most are unaware of and the rest in denial of; this life is not about you. It does, however, include you. Our Lord and Savior came to this world full of grace and truth to create in us a new heart. Why? Man's heart is despicably wicked, and he cannot stand before a Holy and righteous God in his current state. Humanity lies to themselves and others and habitually tells lies to God. Life and death are in the power of the tongue; this truth predicted the downfall of humanity, the inability to control his tongue, and what proceeds from it (Proverbs 18:21). The Bible says that your words will justify and condemn you (Matthew 12:37). Everyone is a witness for or against himself in the Kingdom of God. Every idle word you haven't repented of and for has power against you for judgment. Two of the biggest problems we have in the church today are 1.) we have no idea over the gravity of what we say, and 2.) we exercise no control, accountability, or responsibility for the filthy things coming from our tongues. We have convinced ourselves that we have a right or that it is godly to speak our minds to the detriment of our eternal soul. Therefore, the grace of God found only in Christ Jesus allows humanity to choose life and not death through His solo act of dying in our place. Only upon the steadfast belief and subsequent witness to the existence of the One and Only the Son of God, through repentance of sins, can anyone experience salvation. No single testimony is valid naturally in a court of law or the spiritual realm. As it is in the worldly court of law, you must produce at least one witness to validate or corroborate the validity of a thing.

The Fifth Expose: It Takes Two

Understanding the concept of the Kingdom witness will allow you to see the many instances throughout the Holy Scriptures where the principle of "it takes two" has always been a vital and critical element, spiritually and naturally. In the Garden of Eden, The Lord our God Himself identified it was not good for man to be alone and created for him a suitable helper (Genesis 2:18). Christ Jesus sent the disciples out two by two to proclaim the Kingdom of God to the Jews (Luke 10:1). The concept of two is in everything; good or bad, right, or wrong, day and night, up or down, and hot or cold. Two can establish what a thing is and is not. Two can also depict an addition, agreement, or disparity between two compared objects. Listed below are some of the uses of the "it takes two" principles.

- Those who keep the commandments of God and have the testimony of Christ Jesus (Revelation 12:17)

- Spirit and truth (John 4:24)

- He who is not with me is against me, and he who does not gather with me scatters (Matthew 12:30)

- Saved by the blood of the Lamb and the power of their testimony (Revelation 12:11)

- Chosen and faithful (Revelation 17:14)

- Not only blood but water (1 John 5:6)

- Confess with your mouth Jesus is Lord, and believe in your heart God raised Him from the dead (Romans 10:9)

- Righteousness and justice are the foundations of your Kingdom (Psalms 89:14)

- Heaven or hell (Revelation 20: 15)

- Life or death (Romans 6:23)

What is certain is unless you have a credible witness, namely the Holy Spirit, you will not be entering the Kingdoms of God or heaven. The most terrifying words imaginable to any believer should be the words spoken by Christ Jesus on His judgment day. "Depart from me, you workers of lawlessness. I never knew you," (Matthew 7:23). Our Lord and Savior came to earth in the flesh, lived a sinless life, and died for the sins of the world to make sure you know the truth (John 8:32). You will live and not die somewhere in one of two places. The choice is yours.

Envision the Promise: "But you will receive power when the Holy Spirit comes on you, and you will be my witnesses in Jerusalem, and in all Judea and Samaria, and to the ends of the earth," (Acts 1:8).

KAP IT PRECEPT II

E³ART³H SUIT VS NICHE

The First Expose: E³ART³H SUIT

An anonymous person once said, "Keep following the facts until you get to the truth. If we are to get any better as True Believers, we must face the dark side of humanity. Humans prefer to trust their imaginations rather than lose control by acknowledging the truth. The human imagination has created areas of great concern throughout humankind's existence that is not honest, holistic, or grounded in the truth. I intentionally specify "True Believers" because, as with everything God made good on this earth, it eventually, in time, gets compromised. So, if your hope is somehow divided between your flesh, this world, and its systems, this life, unfortunately, what you currently see is as good as it gets.

This KAP IT precept, **E³ART³H SUIT** vs. **NI⁴C²HE**, is designed to motivate and equip you from reliance on anything that has you clinging to your flesh nature to faith in a spiritual glorified body and home that is unseen. You were first exposed to the term **E³ART³H SUIT** in detail in Chapter Two, *Delusions of Grandeur*, to inform some and remind others that you are not who you think you are. This **E³ART³H SUIT** you placed all your trust in WILL fail to

217

revive itself one day, and the only proven method of salvation and rest for your soul is Christ Jesus. The Bible says that if anyone thinks of himself to be something when he is nothing, he deceives himself (Galatians 6:3). Individuals who don't have an honest and grounded worldview of who they are in Christ Jesus, as their Lord and Savior, and who they are without the Holy Spirit leading and guiding them in these dark days will never experience rest for their souls. These individuals will constantly remain deceived, in denial, or somewhat delusional about their worth, purpose, and duties in this short life. We've already discussed playing Russian roulette with your eternity is not a viable option. Eternity is forever, and there's no coming back from it. That's not what I say. That's what the Word of God says, and belief in God means that if He said it, then it is profitable for you to believe it.

The Second Expose: No Hope and No Rest

Living in this up-and-down life on earth is often tricky and full of adversity (John 16:33). In Chapters One and Two, it was critical, to begin with, the importance of knowing God, followed by learning some not-so-pleasant things about yourself. True Believers have something irreplaceable and vital to survival that the world doesn't have. That would be HOPE. This representation introduced some and reminded others that God does not change, has the authority and right to do as He pleases, and is the author and finisher of what we have coined as the flip side. This principle and understanding will help us transition into God's Emotional Intelligence, which is coined the C.P.E. of God for this work. God's compassion, passion, and empathy (C.P.E.) are His emotional state that is always one hundred percent consistent. God's judgments are true and righteous because He is not human, made of flesh, but a Spirit who created and owns the universe, earth, and everything it contains. He is the perfect King having no futile control issues, human tendencies, fluctuating emotions, or a selfish flesh nature compromised at every level of maturation. Indeed, He is God of all and does Everything He says. Therefore, our hope in the Word of God and His promise of eternal life by faith is worth more than gold and more comforting than any religion in existence. We praise and worship God for His superior C.P.E. that gives us peace of mind. The C.P.E. of God includes the following: The compassion of God (for His people) (John 10:29),

The passion of God (for His name and His word) (Isaiah 55:11)

The empathy of God (found in Christ Jesus) (John 3:16).

Many have problems understanding what the perfect will of God is for their lives as it pertains to their purpose on this earth. God repeatedly expresses His desire for all to live not apart but with Him (Ezekiel 33:11). However, God's perfect will and His permissive will does not detract from the responsibility of each one to choose life or death (Deuteronomy 28:28). This misunderstanding of His perfect will is further complicated by how we operate in these "E³ART³H " suits. As we discussed in Chapter Two, E³ART³H suit is an honest Biblical assessment and sober worldview of our short existence in this world in this flesh. The most important thing to understand about your future is this life is not about your will but includes you and your choices in one of two possible scenarios: either with God or the other, in opposition to God. The only hope you have for your life and future in the latter option is summed up here E³ART³H SUIT.

E³ART³H suit, recapped here to show you the side-by-side differences between this earthly natural house, its limitations, and the home God in Christ Jesus and the power of the Holy Spirit has prepared for all who believe.

Expendable: God loves you; this is true because He gave up His only Son for believers of the True Church to live with Him in eternity. Now the flip side, if your last name isn't A.D. (after death) or B.C. (before Christ) and time itself is not divided by your life and death, you are expendable.

Further, given all your resources, wealth, and worldly knowledge, the realization is you still don't own a place called heaven or hell to place yourself or anyone else. In that case, just like the previous, you can consider yourself expendable (Isaiah 40:17).

Expiring: Unless you have the power to cancel your predetermined date with your box, you have an expiration date. Every individual has a date known to God alone when he will shed this **E³ART³H SUIT**. The Bible speaks to the brevity of this earthly life in the flesh, acknowledging we are like the grass, a mist, or a passing shadow. Wisdom understands that this life is short, and we should strive to make the most of our time here, pleasing in the sight of God, (1 Peter 1:24).

Excommunicated: Every human being, after the fall of Adam and Eve in the Garden of Eden, has succumbed to a sinful nature. God's grace and dominion, which initially shielded and gave authority to Adam over all things on earth in that day, remain revoked because of sin (Genesis 3:17). The only way to reverse or remove this curse is through the blood and finished work of Christ Jesus on the cross. Through one man's sin, all sinned, and through one Man's obedience, many will be made righteous (Romans 5:19).

Unless you have accepted Christ Jesus as your Lord and Savior, you are still excommunicated and at the wrath of God (Romans 5:19).

Artificial: This generation is intimately familiar with fake or artificial goods and services that dictate many facets of how one lives and values their life. The name brand and typically more expensive goods and services are considered more valuable because of their quality and uniqueness. The difference between a twenty-five-dollar pair of jeans and a hundred-and-fifty-dollar pair of jeans sometimes boils down to a name.

Spiritually, you are not the version of who and what you were originally designed for because you lost your name. Initially, Adam was the son of God, made in His likeness and image, and his offspring were likewise to be God's children. Adam and Eve's disobedience produced seeds that, like themselves, were contaminated by sin. Unless one is spiritually reborn of water and Spirit, the fate of humankind will remain in its artificial state. When Adam and Eve sinned against God, everyone born afterward was considered the son of man, not God. The finished work on the cross is the only way humanity could regain its sonship (Genesis 3:16-17).

Remodeled: The fact that we are precious but expendable, definitely expiring naturally, excommunicated, and have an artificial sinful nature leaves us to reason that remodeling has occurred. All humankind has suffered a C4D5 chronic affliction that, if left untreated, will separate him from fellowship with the Lord for eternity. The C4 conditions that compromise, contaminate, corrupt, and endanger humankind with condemnation are the source of the remodeling. This conditioning, in turn, created a D5 disposition in humanity prone to distractions, deception, desensitization, denial of the truth, and disillusion. The water and blood of Christ Jesus covered man's sinful nature and washed away contaminated man's flesh (Genesis 3:22).

Temporary. Everything seen is fleeting, and nothing in this life lasts forever except for the Word of God (Matthew 24:35).

This truth is incredibly transparent regarding flesh and blood, the physical makeup of our mortal bodies. A man's days are between seventy and eighty years (Psalms 90:10).

Time Sensitive Your body has distinct limitations, none more sobering than its sensitivity to time. We live in the entity called time, and the clock is constantly ticking! Time exists outside of eternity and has a beginning and an end. You cannot afford to make mistakes repeatedly because time is a luxury you have very little of, much less buy, add, or borrow time from others or its Creator, God Himself (Psalms 39:5).

Terminally Ill. The Holy Scriptures say all were born to die once, and the following judgment is the fate of all humanity. That's right, ladies and gentlemen, you were born to die, if not naturally, as some will experience no doubt spiritually. The consequences of our heart disease secured all a predetermined date with a box, and there is no getting around it. All men die once, then judgment (Hebrews 9:27).

House. You can look forward to your next eternal dwelling or where you make your new home forever in anticipation and great joy or with sorrow and regret. Your choices are joy and happiness with Jesus in eternity or weeping and gnashing of teeth with Satan, his angels, death, the grave, hell, in the pit. Your CHOICES now can dictate your eternal destination later that you make in your **E³ART³H** suit (John 14:3).

However, for the True Believers whose life is founded on love, faith, and hope, their eternal future looks much different from this world. This world is not our home; this **E³ART³H suit** of mortal flesh will be replaced by what we call a **"NICHE."**

The Fourth Expose: NI⁴C²HE

The True Believer's hope that gives us energy, excitement, and expectation for the future is that we will inherit a glorified body, just like the one our Lord and Savior returned and ascended in when He was raised from the grave. Upon the expiration of this **E³ART³H SUIT**, we hold to the hope that our next home will be in our **NI⁴C²HE**. The glorified body we will receive has features that far exceed the limitations of the **E³ART³H SUIT**. These attributes are what the Holy Scriptures say about our glorified body. They are as follows:

- New (1 Corinthians 15:38)

- Improved (Philippians 3:21)

- Incorruptible (1 Corinthians 15:42-44)

- Imperishable (1 Corinthians 15:42-44)

- Immortal (1 Corinthians 15:40-54)

- Certified (John 20:27)

- Celestial (Acts 1:9)

- Home (2 Corinthians 5:1)
- Eternity (John 14:3)

NEW: Unlike the body that was corrupted flesh, the new body the True Believer receives lasts forever. The Bible says, for our citizenship is in heaven, from which we also eagerly wait for a Savior, the Lord Jesus Christ, who will transform the body of our lowly condition into conformity to the body of His glorious body, by the exertion of the power that He has even to subject all things to Himself (Philippians 3:20-21).

IMPROVED: It is sown in dishonor; it is raised in glory. It is sown in weakness; it is raised in power. It is sown in a natural body and raised as a spiritual body. There is a natural body, and there is a spiritual body (1 Corinthians 15:43-44)

IMPERISHABLE: So is it with the resurrection of the dead. The body that is sown is perishable; it is raised imperishable. The body that is sown in dishonor is raised in glory. The body that is sown in weakness is raised in power (1 Corinthians 15:42-44).

INCORRUPTIBLE: So, when this corruptible has put on incorruption, and this mortal has put on immortality, then it shall be brought to pass the saying that is written: "Death is swallowed up in victory."

IMMORTAL: So, when this corruptible has put on incorruption, and this mortal has put on immortality, then shall be brought to pass the saying that is written: "Death is swallowed up in victory," (1 Corinthians 15:54)

CERTIFIED: Then He said to Thomas, "Reach your finger here, and look at My hands; and reach your hand *here and* put *it* into My side. Do not be unbelieving but believing." Jesus said to him, "Thomas because you have seen Me, you have believed. Blessed *are* those who have not seen and *yet* have believed," (John 20:27, 29)

CELESTIAL: And while they looked steadfastly toward heaven as He went up, behold, two men stood by them in white apparel, who also said, "Men of Galilee, why do you stand gazing up into heaven? This *same* Jesus, who was taken up from you into heaven, will so come in like manner as you saw Him go into heaven," (Acts 1:9-11).

HOME: The cliche "Home is where the heart is" has a new and inspiring meaning when used in the context of your NICHE. When you give your whole heart to Jesus, you have secured an everlasting home! The Bible says, And if I go and prepare a place for you, I will come again to receive you to Myself; where I am there you may also be (John 14:3).

ETERNITY: This is the habitation of everything that is not physical and material here in the entity called time. To be absent from the body is to be present with the Lord (2 Corinthians 5:8). You will be with me where I am. For thus says the High and Lofty One Who inhabits eternity, whose name is Holy (Isaiah 57:15).

Some people's life issues are because they do not have hope or assurance about what things look like in their immediate or long-term future. Others have a more sinister and diabolical problem; they don't care. The Bible speaks of these three things that remain after all physical and material items have burned up: faith, hope, and love, and of these, love remains the greatest and lone standing (1 Corinthians 13:13).

ENVISION THE PROMISE For this we say to you by the word of the Lord, that we who are alive *and* remain until the coming of the Lord will by no means precede those who are asleep. For the Lord, Himself will descend from heaven with a shout, with the voice of an archangel, and with the trumpet of God. And the dead in Christ will rise first. Then we who are alive *and* remain shall be caught up together with them in the clouds to meet the Lord in the air. And thus, we shall always be with the Lord. Therefore comfort one another with these words (1 Thessalonians 4:15-18).

Everything Has to Be Tested

"Test all things; hold fast what is good," (1 Thessalonians 5:21). Beloved, do not believe every Spirit but test the spirits, whether they are of God because many false prophets have gone out into the world," (1 John 4:1). 'Because you have kept My command to persevere, I also will keep you from the hour of trial which shall come upon the whole world, to test those who dwell on the earth," (Revelation 3:10). 'Examine yourselves as to whether you are in the faith. Test yourselves. Do you not know yourselves that Jesus Christ is in you? Unless, indeed, you are disqualified," (II Corinthians 13:5).

The First Expose: Testing Isn't Optional

People are SI²C³K, and SI²C³K people need testing to determine what is ailing them. SI²C³K is an acronym meaning "Suffering Internal Iniquity from Compromised, Contaminated, and Corrupted Knowledge." The knowledge spoken of here is knowing God and knowing ourselves. Most Christians today don't know who they are and are terrified of finding out they are not who or what they pretend to be. Due to their SI²C³K nature, Christians in this century have built more fake gods and artificial Jesus' role models than anyone can count or remember. As demoralizing or more so, some are frightened that people will find out they are not who they

229

proclaim to be behind the mask they wear at church and when tested. So, in anticipation of having to confront themselves with the truth of who they are, they resort to avoidance, denial tactics, and schemes. Avoidance and denial are two reasons Christians become so offended and go through the four postures of truth so quickly. If someone presents the verifiable truth to you, and this offends you, you need to get tested immediately!

God uses testing more for our benefit than for His. Testing is a gauge used in many facets of our daily lives. You must pass a series of tests before proceeding to the next grade level in any area of higher education. You are evaluated or tested before rising to greater responsibilities and supervisory roles in your career or vocation. Likewise, in the Kingdom of God, we are tested to validate the authenticity of faith. God knows the beginning from the end and has already seen and determined our future. If we are willing participants, things work out for our good. If we rebel and disobey, this leads to a life of hardship and strife. Troubles and tribulations help us discover who we are and build the needed character to complete the good works the Lord has planned for our lives. When we willingly participate in His will, God gives us confidence, like a loving and nurturing Father, to establish His will on earth through His word and approval.

Testing has been necessary from the beginning and will continue to the end of the age (1 Thessalonians 5:21). Adam was tested and failed miserably, allowing sin to enter the world. Abraham was tested and became the father of numerous nations. Most of every generation of the children of Israel tested and failed, even until this day. Jesus tested the seventy disciples, leaving only the original twelve. The church is undergoing testing in five critical areas of our discipleship in these last days will determine our just reward on the judgment day of Christ Jesus. The Bible says after the fire has tested us, we will come out pure as gold. There are five distinct reasons for testing in the lives of His people.

1.) To Humble. The original children of the promise always resorted to their familiar Egyptian slave mindset whenever difficulties, temptations, or trials came among them. Although they repeatedly experienced numerous miraculous interventions from the Lord, they rejected God's omnipotence and faithfulness. The test was the manna God gave them for food. Manna was a delicacy they were unfamiliar with, so they grumbled and murmured against the goodness of God. The lesson is to teach them man does not live by bread alone but by every word that comes from the mouth of God (Deuteronomy 8:16).

2.) Expose hearts. Heart disease is not only the number one killer of the natural man in this world, but it is also the number one cause of death for the untested professed believer. There is nothing you can say to describe the unrepentant human heart except who can know it (Jeremiah 17:9). The intentions of a man, what motivates a man, and what a man will do when he gets an opportunity to achieve his wicked imagination are abominable to the Lord (Proverbs 12:2). Murderers, adulterers, false witnesses, and slanderers all proceed from the heart of man, and its end is death (Matthew 15:19). God destroyed the entire earth except for a few animals and eight people because humanity was violent and always imagining evil in his heart (Genesis 6:5). The children of the promise met a similar fate, unwilling to change their attitudes and submit themselves to God. The entire adult generation died except for Joshua and Caleb in the desert. The primary disease plaguing Christians worldwide today is heart disease. Christians are excellent at doing all of the "church-related activities" regarding their salvation except the primary thing, which is allowing the Lord to create inside of them a pure, clean, and new heart.

3.) Obedience. When God tests our will to obey Him, He is looking for evidence of our trust, faithfulness, loyalty, and belief that He is Who He says He is and will do what He says

He will do. Love and obedience are connected and go hand in hand in the Kingdom of God. Jesus says all who love me will obey my commands (John 14:15). Contrary to popular beliefs, the flip side is your love for God is not your earthly, fleshly, and fluctuating feelings. The test of a person's love for God, in Christ Jesus, is in their obedience. The believers' life consists of being tested at intervals, seasons, and times throughout their life to situations and then monitoring their responses as witnesses for or against them. The totality of this testing proves whether you will keep God's commands or not.

4.) Identity. Testing involves a high level of faith and discipline from the believer. To be a son of God is to understand and accept that discipline is a necessary and vital element of your discipleship. The Bible is clear that the rejection of correction is death (Proverbs 12:17). This truth is seen throughout the Bible, beginning in the Garden of Eden with Adam and Eve (Genesis 3:19). The (Fruit) Tree of Knowledge was forbidden to eat, and the known consequences were sure death if they disobeyed. We all know how that ended up for the rest of humanity. Instead of being sons of God, we became sons of man because man's seed had become contaminated because of sin. Later in the history of God's chosen vessels, Abraham, the Father of our Faith, was told to take his only son to the mountain for sacrifice. Abraham's obedience to the test set the stage for the lineage of God's chosen people throughout eternity.

5.) Dependence on God. We can do nothing without God! Man is quick to take credit for things God alone allowed, did, or orchestrated in our lives through His goodness and not by our obedience and faithfulness, which is weak and fluctuating at best. This fluctuating allegiance is why we True Believers are saved by faith alone, not works. Our works would never suffice the price needed to redeem us; only the blood of the Lamb of God could satisfy this debt. Another point of salvation through grace through faith alone is that no man could boast of his work before God because all rightfully suffer from sinful nature. The Bible says, "The eyes of the Lord search the earth so that God can show his loyalty to whoever's heart is loyal and faithful to Him," (2 Chronicles 16:9).

"Let us test and examine our ways and turn back to the Lord,"
(Lamentations 3:40). There are no exceptions; to receive the Kingdom of God, we must come to grips with who we are, so we need to check ourselves. Humankind is prone to search for and depend on things other than God. From the beginning to this day, the same people who cry out for God

one minute are the same worshiping people, money, races, guns, flags, and other idols made and not the Creator.

We don't do things because we are so good. Good is who God is and not our earthly human justification of what we consider good work unto God in His Kingdom. God's definition of good work is faith in His one and only Son Christ Jesus, and obedience to what He says to do as His Church. The few good things we get right are because we have rules, boundaries, integrity, and honesty, which are all characteristics of the Kingdom of God, not human will. The human default setting is ease, convenience, pleasure, and deflection of anything that comes against the previously mentioned! The problem with many is they don't believe God can still love and use them despite their depraved condition because they would not even put up with themselves, much less others. We must empty ourselves of everything but the Kingdom of God and refocus the church on Jesus and His will for His Church and not the divided and divisive entities we have been patronizing on Sundays here in the US and abroad, and this begins with testing.

If anyone claims to know God yet considers themselves to be wiser than God in any way, shape, or form, they have misread the Bible entirely. Man has continually tried to manipulate God with his fake spirituality, part-time allegiance, and loyalty to a self-centered world. Humanity repeatedly finds itself semiconscious of God's actual knowledge because of his heart's imagination. Two things are impossible for humans: 1.) hiding from God and 2.) avoiding judgment for everything you have not repented of in this EARTH suit. God in Christ Jesus will search the heart of every man for their motivations, intentions, and opportunities to give them their due reward (Revelation 2:23).

The Holy Scriptures promise that if we keep the Lord's word to patiently endure, He will keep us from the hour of trial coming upon the whole world to test all who live on the earth (Revelation 3:10). The bottom line is if you don't submit to testing now, you will still have to do it later. If you wait until later, it's not going to be pretty. The Bible says trials and tribulations that will come in that day will be much more challenging than anything ever seen, or ever will see in the future (Matthew 24:21-22).

Envision the Promise: "Consider it all joy, my brethren, when you encounter various trials, knowing that the testing of your faith produces patience" (James 1:2-3).

Chapter Eleven
WHO'S YOUR DADDY?

"Yet for us there is one God, the Father, of whom are all things, and we for Him; and one Lord Jesus Christ, through whom are all things, and through whom we live," (1 Corinthians 8:6). "You cannot drink the cup of the Lord and the cup of demons; you cannot partake of the Lord's table and the table of demons," (1 Corinthians 10:21). "Then God said, "Let us make man in Our image according to Our likeness," (Genesis 1:26). "You are of your father the devil, you want to carry out his desires, he was a murderer from the beginning," (John 8:44).

The First Expose: Heavenly Father

Who's your daddy? The Bible says, "A son honors his father and a servant his master. If then, I Am the Father, where is My honor? And if I Am a Master, where is My reverence? says the Lord of Hosts to you priest who despises my name. Yet you say, in what way have we despised your name?" (Malachi 1:6). The point the Lord made here and quite frankly from the very onset of the entire Bible from man's first presence on the earth is accountability. It was a lack of

237

accountability then, and it is still about an unreasonable standard of accountability in this present age. During the time of Malachi, a prophet and a priest, hundreds of years before Christ Jesus was born, he spoke to deaf ears and dealt with a long heritage of God's people who forsook his laws, commands, statutes, and ordinances. These priests and prophets of his day showed no accountability to God, allowing and condoning the children of God to fall farther and farther away instead of closer to their God. It was their primary job to teach people the ways of God, yet they, although knowing the will of God, sinned against God and taught the children of the promise to disregard the will of God, modeling their rebellion and disobedience. Given the command not to eat of the Tree of Knowledge of good and evil in the middle of the garden, the first man, Adam, the son of God, took no accountability to rebuke Eve, the first lady, for partaking of the forbidden fruit (Genesis 3:6). The aftermath ensued, and humanity paid the price of this consensual act, unleashing what we now know as sin. Sin and its consequence, the death of this earthly flesh vessel, became the fate of all born to man. God would implement a plan using His Only Begotten Son, Jesus Christ, at an appropriate time to fix the entire situation alone through His life and ultimately, death on the cross. The children of the promise relied on natural genetics unsuccessfully time and time again, instead of the Word of God. Despite being taught by the elders, begged by the priests, and chastened repeatedly by God through His prophets about their character and behavior flaws, they obeyed half-heartedly with no sustained progress. Fast forward, upon confrontation with Jesus, these legitimate Jews by birth insisted on their rights as heirs, in futility to the only hope they had right in front of their faces. Jesus corrected them with the truth, stating that they did not walk in the ways of Abraham, their professed father, and the God Abraham worshipped, therefore making them illegitimate sons because they lacked belief in the prophesied One and only Son of God. The truth of their illegitimacy infuriated some of these Jewish descendants and hardened their hearts even more, provoking them to murder. Christ Jesus said, "I will not leave you as orphans; I will come to you," (John 14:18). This statement is critical to understanding who your real dad is in the Spirit because those who accept the Son receive the Father and the Holy Spirit, (John 15:26). Accepting Christ Jesus means submitting your will and sacrificing your body to Christ Jesus as your Lord and Savior. It all boils down to one question about your life that produces eternal ramifications. Will your life be acceptable to God? The way you receive and answer this question in your spirit will tell you a lot about the actual condition of your heart. You have learned that truth offends more than lies.

You can disregard a lie, but you can never run away from the truth, especially in these last days, if discussions about the legitimacy of your salvation or sanctification progress offend you. Check your heart. Claiming Christ Jesus as your Lord and Savior means the rest of your life is dedicated and devoted to the terms and conditions of the Kingdom of God. The Bible says, "God is a Spirit, and those who worship Him must worship Him in spirit and truth (John 4:24). In the Kingdom of God, it's not what you say, for the Kingdom of God is not a word but power," (1Corinthians 4:20). Your actions and the "good things" you seemingly do, do not necessarily validate you as a Child of God any more than being a genetically legitimate blood Jew validates you if you have not been reborn of Spirit and water. For example, Judas was one of the original twelve disciples doing all the works of God but never honestly having the heart of God in Christ Jesus and eventually betraying Him to the death. On judgment day, everyone, dead, dead in Christ, or alive, will be tested to assess the condition of their heart and mind (Jeremiah 17:10). Judgment will determine the sincerity of your witness as a disciple and a follower of Christ Jesus. Jesus said, "You would know them by their fruit." He didn't say by what they say and what they do, but fruit speaks more to the motive, intention, and opportunities in which they performed their works, service, or deed. When God in heaven, in Christ

240

Jesus, and the power of the Holy Spirit abides in you, the
True Believer, your life produces good fruit, and you glorify
your Father in heaven. You don't go to hell because God sent
you there. You go to hell because you fail to comply with the
Word of God, choosing either this world and its stuff or your
daddy, the prince of this world who has already been
condemned and judged. All who follow him will go where he
is forever.

The Second Expose: Your Natural Father

What happened to the natural fathers missing, dead,
imprisoned, non-existent, or gone AWOL in the world today?
In the United States, this question has been the topic of many
studies and possibly more knowledgeably answered fifty years
ago than today. Today's generation believes covering up a
truth and replacing it with their less offensive version of the
truth is somehow Christian. According to the US Census
Bureau, as studied by the National Fatherhood Initiative, 18.3
million children live without a biological, step, or adoptive
father in the home (National Fatherhood Initiative). The
study showed that this contributed to a four times greater risk
of poverty, seven times more likelihood of teenage
pregnancy, behavioral problems, the tendency to abuse drugs
and alcohol, and several other potential short and long-term
adverse effects. This phenomenon is separate and, in addition

to the internal civil unrest that exists and spreads rampantly in this country.

These escalating events caused an already racially and economically divided country to fall into perils, pre-voting rights, and civil rights acts of the mid-1960s in comparison. There are many problems and far too few viable solutions for the melting pot, the self-proclaimed Christian Capital of the world, the United States of America (USA). The citizens, immigrants, and the world continue to watch daily as the tension mounts between the government, the US citizens, and the religious community amidst the eye-opening disparity, partiality and hypocrisy undeniably tearing this country and nation apart. Follow the blood whenever you want to find the truth of any matter. The last posture in the four stages of biblical truth is murder. It has been that way from the beginning. From its very onset, hypocrisy and partiality have been the modus operandi of the United States, inciting oppression, persecution, and bloodshed throughout its history. The world witnessed much horrific truth covering a span of the last four hundred years in the US, which looks nothing remotely like the Kingdom of God on earth. The United States has slowly been revealed in an unbecoming fashion and has come to the point of reckoning. Jesus is at the door knocking, but many haven't answered the call. Or maybe no one is at home. Jesus said to the children of Israel, claiming to be the children of the promise, "You are of your father the devil because you do the desires of your father," (John 8:44). So, I ask the USA again, "Who is your daddy?" Hopefully, the point becomes clear to you as we dive deeper into this chapter and possibly shed some light on why there is so much division, strife, persecution, oppression, unrest, and no peace in any way, shape, or form in this country. We discussed this subject earlier in Delusions of Grandeur; you reap what you sow. Do you think God would sweep under the rug all the hurt, killing, and stealing over the last four hundred years? What is done in the dark will come to light; what is said secretly will be shouted from the rooftops (Luke 12:3). The heart of America has been placed front and center for testing and has failed dramatically. Let us look at why.

The definition of the Kingdom of God is **God's accepted, and man's approved spiritual will of joy, peace, and righteousness in the Holy Spirit reflected through His church on this earth that gives the power to influence whosoever wills character (thoughts, attitudes, and behaviors) in service to Christ Jesus.** As we begin to break down the Kingdom of God piece by piece, scripture by scripture, you will start to see where this country many have placed in such false high esteem, hiding behind an appearance of truth and freedom for all, only recognizes the rich and wealthy. Some knowingly, many unknowingly, have fallen miserably short of who and what they claim to believe. The spiritual Kingdom of God is described below:

1. God's accepted: There are only two on earth alone that are acceptable to God the Father as far as salvation and sanctification are concerned on this earth. To seek eternal life, you need two things, Jesus for salvation (John 3:16) (John 14:14) and the One Like Him, the Holy Spirit, for sanctification. The Holy Spirit is not an option. You are sealed unto redemption by the Holy Spirit, which means He keeps you until Jesus returns to gather His church.

2. Man's approved. The delusion that a person loves God yet is unwilling to love his brothers and sisters in Christ Jesus is prevalent in this age. The same God who said, "Love your Lord your God with all your heart, mind, and strength gave the same command to love your neighbor as yourself," (Mark 12:30-31). Honoring all people, treating others better than yourselves, and having peace with all as much as it pertains to yourself is the will of God for His chosen people. There is no loophole; if you hate your brother, you are, by the Word of God, a murderer, and no murderer will enter the Kingdom of God (1 John 3:15).

3. Spiritual Will. The natural will of man directly opposes his spiritual will due to his human, fallen nature. Sin contaminated the perfect man God made. Humanity's natural and spiritual will never exist harmoniously. It is one or the other. Walk in the Spirit, and you shall not fulfill the desires of the flesh (Gal 5:16). If we live in the Spirit, let us also walk in the Spirit (Galatians 5:25).

4. Joy. Joy is an emotional contentment working inside a person despite what's happening around or even to that person. The present circumstances or situations one may be experiencing are replaced by a future expectation and hope that makes up for the current inconvenience. Joy can be defined as the victory gained after all is said and done. Joy makes everything worth the sacrifice and perseverance. Happiness, on the flip side, is about you and temporary contentment. Jesus said, "These things I have spoken to you so that my joy will be in you," (John 15:11).

5. Peace, My peace I leave with you, not as the world gives. This is the Peace of God, Peace with God, and Peace in God (OWI Peace). This type is not the temporary peace of the world wrapped in materials and sensual pleasures but peace within because of rest for your souls with eternal life.

6.   Righteousness. This type of righteousness cannot be found in man, but only the righteousness accomplished through the finished work of Christ Jesus on the cross (Matthew 6:33).

7.   Holy Spirit. The Holy Spirit has many names and works inside all true believers. Another like Me, the Counselor, Changes Us (Gal 5:22), Comforter (John 14:16-17), teach you all things, (John 14:26) The Spirit of Truth, (John 15:26) Intercession, (Romans 8:26-27, Acts 19:2), "He will remind you of all I had said." The Holy Spirit agrees with our spirit creating a seal unto the True Believer's redemption (Romans 8:6).

8.   Reflected: Our reflection is traits and characteristics that spiritually and legitimately qualify Believers as children of God. You are the light of the earth, a lamp on a hill that cannot be hidden; shine your good deeds before men so that your Father in heaven is glorified (Mat 5:14).

9.   Church: Upon this rock, I will build MY CHURCH, and the gates of hell will not prevail against it (Mat 16:18). These individuals are the called-out people of God in Christ Jesus and sealed by the Holy Spirit.

10. Power: The Kingdom of God is not in word but in power (1 Corinthians 4:20). The power of God is not evident in personal appearances or the overwhelming

charisma of gifted orators and powerful speakers. The power of God is adequately manifested through joy, peace, and righteousness toward God; patience, goodness, and kindness toward others; self-control in your body; meekness in your spirit; and faithfulness in your soul or being (Galatians 5:21-22). These attributes give the True Church power.

11. *Influence:* The gospel of the Kingdom preached to the world seeks to influence people to live and not die! The Holy Scriptures refer to this influence as Spiritual Salt (Matthew 5:13). Salt is a natural preservative and metaphorically used by our Lord Christ Jesus as an attribute of how we should impact this world.

12. *Whosoever wills*: For God so loved the world that whosoever believe in Him shall not perish but have everlasting life. In this dispensation of grace, all have a choice to choose salvation.

13. *Character* (thoughts, attitudes, behaviors) (Genesis 1:26)
    The children of God bare His likeness (character) and image (function, behavior).

14. *In-Service* (Romans 14:17) There is no getting around it; either you are a servant of Christ Jesus or a willing participant in the enemy's camp (Matthew 12:30). Your life work and the fruit displayed in your EARTH suit will

decide your allegiance. Jesus said anyone who serves Me him My Father will honor, (John 12:26). The difference between meager existence in this life and an exuberant life to come is predicated on your commitment to service.

15. *To Christ Jesus* (Romans 14:18) There is only One name in heaven or earth that all things have become subject to as Supreme and the Overcomer of death and the grave. While teaching the importance of forgiveness, Christ Jesus identified himself on judgment day as the officer and His heavenly Father as the judge.

Your earthly father and family structure greatly influence your natural and spiritual training. The Bible says to train up a child in the way he should go, and when he is old, he will not depart from it (Proverbs 22:6). This way of life benefits a successful and fulfilling life on earth and assurance through hope and faith in the next life in eternity. The enemies have derailed and eroded the family unit. Curses are the consequences or flipside of blessings associated with rebellion and disobedience to the known will of God.

America as a professed leader of morality today, for some immoral, some societal, but all equally debilitating reasons, has suffered these curses. The absence of fathers presents a unique challenge for today's child, producing individuals missing the vital emotional and homogeneous structure a growing child needs to function in society adequately. The family, the community, and the nation, especially with this generation of adolescents primarily raised in a social media influenced environment, impact the mother with undue hardships, often emotionally, psychologically, and physically through stress. Fatherless homes affect the community and nation because of the negative consequences that plague single-parent homes with issues such as children who are more likely to abuse drugs and alcohol, have behavioral problems and have a four times greater risk of poverty (National Fatherhood Initiative). The Bible says you were once dead because of your failures and sins. You followed the ways of this present world and its spiritual ruler. This ruler continues to work in people who refuse to obey God (Ephesians 2:1-2). One visible sign of our natural EARTH suit and spiritual nature is our identification by sharing likeness (character) or image (our function or behaviors)(Genesis 1:26). There are several fathers mentioned in the Bible, our earthly, natural fathers, spiritual fathers, The Heavenly Father, the only legitimate father, and then there is one more; the father of lies.

The Third Expose: Father of Lies

In the end, ladies and gentlemen, you will spend eternity with the father that you alone chose to worship. The Father of

Lies, Satan, Jesus says, was a liar and a murderer from the beginning, and there is no truth in him (John 8:44). He further explained, "You are of your father the devil; he was a liar from the beginning." This statement was a critical concept Jesus attempted to teach the fish sandwich kids of His time. Again, they are referred to as the "fish sandwich" generation because they denied the true bread, Christ Jesus, merely following Him for perishable bread and fish that filled their bellies. This generation rejected His word, the only source of eternal life, focusing on their earthly wants and desires, knowing there is a life after our mortal existence. The lesson to be learned by these people is their biological makeup or being Hebrew pure Jews to the blood in their ancestry still did not qualify them as the children of God. Their only qualification at that time or today is total surrender to our Lord and Savior, Jesus Christ. The "fish sandwich" generation had to shift their full belief and trust from their works and heritage onto Him as the Son of God sent down as the Savior of the entire world just as it was written of Him. However, in addition to faith, there should be some form of life change, work, or deeds that reflect what a person says they believe. The evidence of a person's faith is his work displayed through his thoughts, attitudes, and behaviors (James 2:26). The works that reflect evidence of true salvation are repentance for our sins and genuine love for one another. All iniquities, transgressions, and rebellions are covered by faith for anyone who confesses and truly believes. The repeated behavior in the history of God's chosen people consistently involves some form of rejection and then an outpouring of repentance. Just as they rejected God and His Prophets ending with John the Baptist, the message was consistently about the King in the line of David that was to come. After John the Baptist, Jesus the prophesied King, bearing of Himself with signs and wonders no other man had ever performed, was not only rejected but blamelessly murdered. Jesus the Christ, after the completion of His ministry, unbeknown to the people he came to minister to, needed to choose whether they would receive Him and salvation or reject Him and still be lost and condemned in their sins.

Children of the flesh have not been reborn of the Spirit and water, which is the defining factor of genuinely being a child of God. Their behavior reflects that they are still willing to participate in things unacceptable to God and His divine will for our lives to live with him eventually. The Bible says the works of the flesh are evident, including adultery, fornication, uncleanness, lewdness, idolatry, sorcery, hatred, contentions, jealousy, outburst of wrath, selfish ambition, dissensions, heresies, envy, drunkenness, and revelries. These things dominate our culture and society today, calling them fundamental rights, despite the offense they pose to the Kingdom of God.

All these thoughts, attitudes, and behaviors through belief in Jesus Christ, who shed His blood and died to redeem you and remove the burden of guilt, judgment, and condemnation, all by confession and repentance. When you accept Christ Jesus, your sins are forgiven and symbolically nailed to the same cross Christ Jesus died upon through your faith and belief in Him alone. The Father sent Jesus so that we might escape death and the grave and live eternally with Him forever, with and in us His children called by His Holy name who love Him and are the called according to the purposes He alone has for our lives.

The Fourth Expose: Children of God. We are either children of God or children of the flesh. Being children of God means we are reborn spiritually (belief) into His likeness (character) and His image (behavior), no longer living out our daily lives with no accountability to God because we know Him. We first must believe in God as the One True God, the creator of heaven, earth, and everything seen and unseen in it. We believe and accept Christ Jesus as the only begotten Son of God, being God Himself, coming to earth wrapped in the flesh to save the entire world in our sin, through the belief in His name "Christ Jesus" alone. We understand that it is only by grace through faith in the finished work of Jesus Christ alone on the cross that we now have the opportunity for salvation (Ephesians 2:8-9). As children of God to the one who we understand that unless we receive the Holy Spirit possessing its sanctification, power, work, and witness in our lives, we are not true children of God. We must also accept discipline, which includes suffering and its work to perfect us into the image of Christ Jesus, who is the first of His kind who suffered and died so that we might live eternally with Him. If we do not accept discipline, the Bible says we are illegitimate children (Hebrews 12:8) because God corrects the ones He loves. As His children, we exhibit humility, self-control, and faith, which are the fruit of the Spirit that gives us the power to seek to do the things in Christ Jesus that are good, acceptable, and perfect in the sight of God.

The Fifth Expose: The Lord Knows Whose Is His

The Spirit Himself bears witness that we are children of God with our spirit. As we discussed in Chapter Ten, "It Takes Two, The Power of Your Witness," nothing of its own is admissible as truth without the confirmation of a witness. In the New Covenant initiated by our Lord and Savior Christ Jesus through his voluntary death for all humanity's sins, The Lord our God received His perfect unblemished sacrifice. This lone act of obedience provided once and for all time the removal of sins of the entire world for whoever believed in Him as their Lord and Savior. Through obedience to God, a believer would receive the promise of the Holy Spirit, thereby sealing them unto redemption or the return of our Lord and Savior Christ Jesus.

You can't live like the world and be a part of God's eternal Kingdom. Jesus forewarned us that the Kingdom of God does not work that way! Everyone has a choice; our life here on earth is simply this, deciding where you want to spend eternity because it's totally up to you.

Envision the promise: Yet for us, there is one God, the Father, of whom are all things, and we for Him; and one Lord Jesus Christ, through whom are all things, and through whom we live (1 Corinthians 8:6).

Chapter Twelve
DNA TESTING

"But ye shall receive power, after that the Holy Ghost comes upon you: and ye shall be witnesses unto me both in Jerusalem, and in all Judaea, and in Samaria, and unto the uttermost part of the earth," (Acts 1:8). "But you are not in the flesh but in the Spirit if indeed the Spirit of God dwells in you. Now, if anyone does not have the Spirit of Christ, he is not His. And if Christ is in you, the body is dead because of sin, but the Spirit is life because of righteousness," (Romans 8:9-10).

The First Expose: DNA

Chapter One, The Flip Side, introduced us to the two categories of people in this world, the natural man and the spiritual man. The absence or the presence of the Holy Spirit in a person's life is the validating factor differentiating these two types of individuals. Salvation and sanctification of the body is foolishness to the natural man, while it is life, light, and peace to the spiritual man (1 Corinthians 2:14-15). The absence of the Holy Spirit, regardless of the person's religious or non-religious background, creates a spiritual "disposition of no authority," or what this work identifies as Spiritual

DNA. Spiritual DNA is used as an analogy to correlate the natural biological structure of deoxyribonucleic acid or DNA to the necessity of the Holy Spirit in a person's life now. This unique genetic code makes up all living things. The Holy Spirit is vital because all True Believers must possess it to be in Christ Jesus for salvation (John 3:5).

Humans, plants, and animals contain their type of DNA relative to their kind and species. Likewise, the Holy Spirit is the gift from God provided through the birth, life, death, and resurrection of our Lord and Savior, Jesus Christ, that all True Believers receive (Acts 2:38). The Holy Spirit provides the True Believer with a disposition of power over his natural desires, authority over his enemies, and access to eternal life and spiritual riches in this world and the next (Luke 11:13). The natural person, contrarily, lives life with a "disposition of no authority" (DNA) that exists with little or no spiritual understanding. The natural man is ignorant and denies accountability even after acknowledging the inevitable physical death on this earth. The natural man must constantly be visually motivated and incentivized while operating extensively through fluctuating emotions and feelings. The natural man exists primarily in a pleasure-seeking, self-preserving worldview, and state of being.

A testament to the incredible knowledge and wisdom of our God is that of the approximate 117 billion people who have ever lived on earth, not one was a hundred percent alike, yet we all share 99.9 percent of the same biological makeup (Kaneda and Haub). Keep in mind that the chemical ratio of humans differs based on race, but the types of minerals are all consistent (Toledo and Saltsman). This science is powerful biblical truth because the Bible says we were all made of "one blood," (Acts 17:27). These DNA strands equip organic matter to reproduce after their kind. In humans specifically, there's a process called DNA testing that allows people to find out exactly who is in their biological family ancestry. Your DNA gives you your makeup and design, following your birth mother and father in your family ancestry. Correspondingly, the absence of the Holy Spirit is the defining spiritual element separating the natural man from the spiritual man relative to his spiritual genetic makeup (faith, beliefs, etc). To further understand the consequences of operating in the world view of the natural man and the benefits of living in the Spirit, we must first understand who can and who cannot receive the Holy Spirit. Second, we need to know what it takes to maintain and sustain the Spirit in an individual's daily walk, and third, what it looks like when working as it should in a True Believer's life.

The Second Expose: Spiritually Deficient

There are two reasons why people of this world and generations suffering from Spiritual DNA cannot receive the Holy Spirit and its power to live and work in one's daily life. The first reason is the self-evident condition of the natural man, that truthfully identifies that he does not know God; therefore, he, in turn, does not know the Son of God, the One God has sent (John 3:16). Knowing God is a prerequisite to first knowing Jesus because the Bible says that unless the Lord draws a person to the Son of God, he cannot receive Him (John 6:44). Though the people God chose, these Jewish descendants, by birth, were anxiously waiting on the prophesied Messiah to arrive, He stood right in front of them, and they never recognized Him. Likewise, today, even with a fully completed Bible and technology more sophisticated than in any other period in world history, the world and believers alike are still getting it wrong.

The second reason the world and this generation cannot receive the Holy Spirit is that they cannot see Him. There are two aspects to this point. Naturally, the world can't receive Him because they do not accept anything they can't visually put their eyes on despite all the invisible attributes that exist today. The wind, the air you breathe daily, thoughts, energy, love, and the list go on, but the worldly mind stays far away from an invisible and all-powerful God. The second aspect is seeing is symbolic in the Bible for understanding. As was first stated, the natural person cannot perceive spiritual things. The Bible says the world views the cross as foolish because they are perishing, but it is eternal life for us who believe (1 Corinthians 1:18).

Our Lord and Savior said there are only sheep and goats, you are with me or against me, and either you are a scatterer or a gatherer (Matthew 12:30). Because the Holy Spirit only repeats what He has heard, and not of His own authority, (John 16:13) He must follow the same guidelines to the letter as Jesus obeyed His commands given to Him by the Father (John 12:49). There are three possible postures of the Holy Spirit in a believer's life: acceptance, rejecting, or grieving the Holy Spirit.

The Third Expose: Postures of the Spirit

A.) Acceptance. Accepting the Holy Spirit into a believer's life manifests a disposition of wisdom, knowledge, and understanding that gives the power to discern God's will in Christ Jesus needed for the True Believers' sanctification. It is only possible to recognize the hand of the Lord in your life and to discern His will if you have access to the Holy Spirit (John 14:26). The Holy Spirit is the Promise sent by Christ

Jesus after His departure that lives inside every True Believer, leading, directing, and guarding True Believers into all truths.

Acceptance of the Holy Spirit also allows the True Believer to bear fruit and ensure their fruit remains (John 15:6). The fruit of the Spirit is the work produced inside the heart of a True Believer that influences how he interacts with God, with his brothers, neighbors, and even his enemies, and lastly, the self control of his body in service to Christ Jesus (Romans 12:12). Jesus explained that a person whose heart is fixated on envy, vain prayers, and self-righteousness would not receive any credit in heaven and commands believers to do their deeds in secret so that their Father in heaven can be glorified in heaven and reward them openly on earth (Matthew 6:1). Any posture other than accepting the Holy Spirit positions an unbeliever or believer to reject the Holy Spirit or worse grieve the Holy Spirit.

B.) Rejection. Contrarily, a person operates blindly and defenselessly without the Holy Spirit as the source of true wisdom and knowledge, which produces legitimate power over the enemies of this world (Galatians 5:17). Rejecting the Holy Spirit means that a believer has forfeited the power necessary to fight and win the daily spiritual battles waged by the three enemies (flesh, world, and Satan) who war against the souls of all believers. For example, an unbeliever who has now accepted the gospel's good news and gets "baptized," this person "will" be saved (Mark 16:16). This baptism is the acceptance of the Holy Spirit in whom, and because your confession of faith; you have now surrendered your life in service to Christ Jesus. The "will" mentioned above is a flip side word, meaning it is not automatic but a lifelong process. The Holy Spirit works in opposition to our sinful nature that wars against our mind and body to maintain it holy and blameless. The new believers are responsible for crucifying the old person they were before they received the gospel's good news and were baptized in the Holy Spirit (Galatians 5:24).

The problem is many don't want to change and become righteous; they just don't want to burn in hell for eternity (John 3:19). These individuals live a life resisting the Holy Spirit (Acts 7:51) or foolishly rejecting it altogether, called grieving the Holy Spirit, which is the last posture and the last we will discuss.

Rejection of the Holy Spirit creates two debilitating issues in an individual and in the body of Christ as a whole as we attempt to witness to a world overtaken with unbelief, ungodliness, and an appetite for immoral living. The loss of identity and influence over the enemy for the church has been negatively affected because of the lack of accountability to

God and responsibility to Christ Jesus in service, which was professed but not truly believed and working in the believers' life.

The Fourth Expose: Identity Crisis

The Loss of Identity means that there is no distinction between the unacceptable ways of the people of this generation and those who profess to believe and claim salvation. The validating attributes of the Holy Spirit living and working in a person are not always identifiable by what is said or even what they sometimes do; it is their ability to bear fruit and produce works by faith worthy of repentance (James 2:17).

Flesh and blood will not inherit the Kingdom of God! Beginning with our Lord, Christ Jesus (John 3:3), and echoed home by the apostle Paul (1 Corinthians 15:50), there is clarity about interpreting this identity-defining point. Yet, the current church is on the tail end of a two-thousand-year identity crisis. Every conceivable manufactured and cultural attribute, including racial, ethnic, religious denomination, or societal dogma, uses its platform as the acceptable way to access the Kingdom of God. The current church cannot attain its own identity because it constantly is adopting practices and habits the Lord has identified as defiling and abominable and labeling them as Christian and loving. The inability or reluctance to draw a line in the sand as Christ Jesus and the early apostles commanded the first disciples has stagnated separation from the world. Come out from among them, be separate, and touch no unclean thing, were the conditions to be received back into the grace and mercy of the Lord (2 Corinthians 6:17). The Holy Scriptures acknowledge God's will for His people regarding this subject, which has not and will not change (Malachi 3:6).

The Fifth Expose: Power Struggles

The loss of influence happens in the body of Christ as the credibility and authenticity of the gospel's message and power are defiled because it preaches a different Jesus than the one in the Holy Scriptures. This false teaching is coupled and compounded by the infusion of an illegitimate spirit given by the enemy to derail the valid message of the gospel. Only the Holy Spirit given by God through Christ Jesus has legitimate power to save souls.

The spirit is willing, but the flesh is weak (Matthew 26:41) is one of the ongoing struggles compromising the current church from the transition into the True Church. Underestimating the power of your fleshly nature is a grave mistake leading unsuspecting church attendees into denial and, subsequently, a false sense of security regarding their salvation and sanctification process. In the flesh-minded capacity, there is no more sobering scripture reference than (Romans 8:6), which states the flesh brings death and the Spirit life and peace. Again, when we recite the scripture reference that flesh and blood cannot inherit the Kingdom of God, it should resonate with an entirely new perspective and prayerful behavior (1 Corinthians 15:50). Dying to your fleshly nature daily is not optional but rather an essential attribute showing God's power in a True Believer's life.

C.) Grieving the Holy Spirit occurs when there is a departure or no presence of the Holy Spirit that previously worked and lived in the believer's life. King David alluded to what this situation might look like in Psalms 51, known as David's Prayer of Repentance (Psalms 51:1-19). King David pleaded with the Lord after committing adultery with Bathsheba and then sending her husband Uriah to the front lines of war, securing Uriah's chances of becoming mortally wounded. When the prophet Nathan confronted David about his sins, he immediately prayed to the Lord God. King David pleaded with the Lord not to cast him away from His presence, take His Holy Spirit away, but to create in him a new heart, restore the joy of his salvation, and renew a right spirit within him and to finally uphold him through His generous Spirit (Psalms 51:10-12).

King David, unlike many today, knew the Lord, and just as importantly, the Lord knew David's heart. Yes, David made a horrible choice and then proceeded to make an even worse choice. Still, David repented immediately and agreed to suffer the consequences of his sins that included, among a list of things, the death of the child conceived through this ungodly relationship and the sword that would not depart his house or lineage (2 Samuel 12:10,14).

Fast forward to the twenty-first century, and according to the new covenant given by Christ Jesus, the Holy Spirit with David now lives within all True Believers. The Bible says all manner of sin will be forgiven, but the blasphemy against the Holy Spirit is unforgivable in this dispensation of grace, and the next dispensation, which is the return of Christ Jesus' eternal reign (Matthew 12:32). As we discussed in Chapter Four, *No Fourth Option*, we now understand there is no other chance for humanity, and refusal to obey the Holy Spirit and to practice things that God in Christ Jesus hates will result in your eternal destruction.

The Sixth Expose: The Work of the Holy Spirit

The work of the Holy Spirit in a True Believer's life allows him to be convicted of three essential elements of our salvation and sanctification processes while waiting for the return of our Lord and Savior to retrieve us and take us where He is forever. The Holy Spirit is the Promise the Lord provided for us regarding our salvation, and it also is the evidence. The Bible says that The Spirit agrees with our spirit that we are the children of the Promise (Romans 8:9) and our seal unto redemption (Ephesians 4:30). The Holy Spirit also acts as a conscience, counselor, or advocate that reminds the True Believer of everything our Lord and Savior Christ Jesus has said (John 14:26).

The Holy Spirit is the wisdom of God that lives inside the True Believer that allows them to do the will of God, who assigned His children "good works" before the foundations of the earth (Ephesians 2:10), to bear fruit that remain (John 15:16), and to be salt and light to an unbelieving world (Matthew 5:13-14). When the True Believer is correctly reflected Christ Jesus through the power of the Holy Spirit living and working in them, the result is the power of God is glorified through and by faith in that individual (Philippians 4:19).

The Bible says I will pour out my Spirit on all flesh and your sons and daughters will prophesy, your old men will dream dreams, young men shall see visions, and the men and women servants of God will also have the power of the Holy Spirit poured on them (Joel 2:28). This same Holy Spirit that leads the children of God into holiness, righteousness, and truth, will convict the world of sin, righteousness, and judgment (John 16:8).

The Seventh Expose: Sin

The first of the three is the conviction of sin because man did not believe God in Christ Jesus. Everyone suffers from the contamination of sinful nature, from Adam and Eve's fall in the garden to the baby being born this very second. Sin has entered all men, a state that results in a genetic disposition that causes us to grow old and die. The Bible has many instances of people seemingly on the outside looking in. All nations that persecuted the children of Israel did so, knowing that the God of Abraham, Isaac, and Jacob was real and consistent. Today, many afflicted individuals suffer from ignorance and denial of their actual state simply because they do not choose to believe, or they do not test themselves at all or regularly for the presence of the Holy Spirit (2 Corinthians 13:5).

The Eighth Expose: Righteousness.

The Holy Spirit convicts the world of righteousness because Jesus has returned to his Father in heaven (John 16:10). Jesus has indeed exited the building called earth. Still, He left us a precious and powerful substitute. The Bible says, "One like

Him," who will be with us forever (John 14:16-17 TPT). This person was the Holy Spirit who lives in us, convicts us, regenerates us, and imparts God's love to all believers. He talks to the Father for us and enables us to bring to remembrance all that the Lord Jesus said and commanded us to do (John 14:26). The Spirit recants God's truth to us while empowering us with gifts to work in the body of Christ, to edify the body. The Fruit of the Spirit prepares us for holy lives, freeing us from sin, leading us in spiritual warfare in the fight against Satan, and convicting us against the world and its ways. The Holy Spirit is our comforter and our encourager.

The Ninth Expose: Judgment

The ruler of this world, the prince of the air, now stands judged (John 16:11). So why do we give him more power to influence our lives than he legitimately has when we know he is a defeated foe? The keys to the grave, death and hell Satan once controlled have now rightfully transferred to the Son of God (Revelation 1:18). The True Believer understands there aren't just one but three potential enemies; Satan, the world, and your flesh nature, which the Holy Bible depicts as enemies of your soul. However, people place ninety-nine percent of the blame on the devil alone. Emphasis is placed primarily on the defeated enemy, the devil, and rightfully so because he ultimately is the author of all disobedience (1 John

3:8). The natural tendencies of humankind, disobedience, rebellion, our iniquities, and corruption are the characteristics of Satan. His committed rebellion against the known will of God resulted in his ejection from the Kingdom of heaven (Luke 10:18). His futile attempt to be like God, seeking worship to fill his pride-infused heart, deceived by his outer beauty, would seal his eternal fate.

Seemingly succeeding in his efforts to influence others to rebel, the devil convinced a third of the angels to rebel with him, and all were cast out of heaven. Christ Jesus came to destroy the works of the devil, and the devil now stands judged, and his reign is all but over (1 John 3:8). The only way we can win this spiritual warfare in these natural bodies is through the indwelling of the Holy Spirit. Without the Holy Spirit (Spiritual DNA), the body of Christ Jesus, the church will continue to suffer massive defeats allowing unrighteousness to thrive and flourish because of our inability to humble ourselves and love our brothers as ourselves.

Righteousness and holiness are a choice one makes after they have had an intimate encounter with the goodness of the Lord. Keep in mind this righteousness that one accepts in his heart is not about anything you did but solely due to the finished work of Christ Jesus on the cross. Any self-righteousness will not suffice the purposes of God (1

Corinthians 1:30). Our Lord and Savior recited a parable describing what makes the Word of God unfruitful in a believer's life. In the parable of the Sower, Jesus depicted four types of soil representing the condition of the heart, three of which had unfruitful outcomes. A critical point the Gospel of Mark records Jesus explaining is that this parable is essential to understanding all other parables. You cannot successfully navigate this life on your own and expect to live eternity with God in Christ Jesus. There are too many enemies for anyone to face in their own strength, especially when one of the enemies lives inside of you!

Envision the Promise Therefore, my beloved brethren, be steadfast, immovable, always abounding in the work of the Lord, knowing that your labor is not in vain in the Lord, (1 Corinthians 15:58).

Chapter Thirteen
C.L.T.T. (CHURCH LEGITIMACY TRAINING & TESTING)

"I know your works, love, service, faith, and your patience; and as for your works, the last are more than the first," (Revelation 2:19). "And they cried with a loud voice, saying, how long, O Lord, holy and true, dost thou not judge and avenge our blood on them that dwell on the earth? 11 And white robes were given unto every one of them; and it was said unto them, that they should rest yet for a little season, until their fellow servants also and their brethren, that should be killed as they were, should be fulfilled," (Revelation 6:10-11).

The First Expose: Church Legitimacy

Church legitimacy refers to being a representative of the one and only True Church, the enduring church created by Christ Jesus, the head of the church body. The church is not a building, but a group of people called out of the world by God to be His special possession (1 Corinthians 6:19). Unfortunately, the message we often hear and see some pastors, teachers, and prophets relay and the example they set for the flock today are sometimes beyond preposterous. In this season, where many leaders of the church exhibit

lifestyles of "do as I say but don't pay attention to what I do,"
immorality, false teaching, and prophesying are more the
norm than the exception. These leaders accepted the call and
then took responsibility for governing the souls of the fold in
preparation for the marriage supper of the Lamb (Revelation
19:9). (When Jesus receives His church to Himself...) All
leaders and teachers, past and present, in charge of God's
children, will be held accountable for the souls they misled
(James 3:1). The duties and responsibilities of the priest of the
Lord are as follows:

- A covenant of life and peace

- Reverence and awe of the Word of God

- True instruction from his mouth

- No lie on his lips

- Walk upright before God and man

- Turn man from sin

- A reservoir of knowledge and fountain of instruction
  (Malachi 2:5-7)

It has shocked me repeatedly in these last three years of
consecration as I have studied and followed many apostles,
pastors, and teachers while studying and training to write this
book of my observations. Almost weekly, not to call any

names, but worth mentioning because of this church's colossal following, unsuspecting people are misled. The fruit of this pastor's hypocrisy, partiality, and ignorance of what this pastor doesn't understand or possibly refuses to acknowledge will mislead the flock. Grievous enough in these last days is the task of avoiding false teachers, but ignorant ones are just as deadly to the spirit and soul. The more attentive I am in this season, the more I hear some teaching elements with critical flaws that could be detrimental to the weak in knowledge and faith. I have listened to a pastor say just recently that there is no such thing as systemic racism despite the history of this country for over four hundred years. I've heard that same pastor tell you there is no such thing as global warming, while the actions of man's irresponsibility to God's creation of water, earth, and air have it undrinkable, polluted, or burning up in front of our eyes. I've heard pastors say there's no such thing as the evil of white supremacy, while countless lives have been lost simply because of the color of someone's skin in a malign attempt at a superior race. I've seen pastors with Confederate flags flying high on their church podcasts, then turn right around and call out others living in idolatry and lacking the love of Christ Jesus. Too often, I've watched pastors teach on tithes, offerings, and giving but somehow leave out the righteousness, mercy, peace, and holy mandate of the

Kingdom of God. Some churches are made up entirely around giving and use their version of the "Good News" message to manipulate people into building structures for the glory of men instead of building people for the tabernacle of God with and in men (Revelation 21:3). The True Church operates on this principle; serving God our creator, through Jesus Christ our Lord and Savior, by the power of the Holy Spirit that lives and works in all true believers and serving others made like us in the likeness and image of God (Matthew 28:19-20). Christ Jesus said, "Unless you follow My example as He washed the disciples' feet, you can have no parts with me" (John 13:8).

Jesus, the Lord, and Savior of the entire world lived a life of humility and service and commanded His followers to do likewise. Though shocking to a few, this statement is true; serving is not about you being a loner, secluded from the rest of the church. Serving one another glorifies our Father in heaven because service is a mandate for Kingdom citizens. The Bible says that our creation is for good works, to live our lives in them (Ephesians 2:10). Every person's end on this side of heaven will be either as a willing servant accepted or the latter, the example of what is unacceptable, one who seeks to be served and you have total autonomy over your fate. God created all things for His glory, and His will for our lives is to serve and please Him (Revelation 4:11).

The Second Expose: Church Training "Church 101"

This current generation, lost and spiritually blind, suffers a distorted Christian worldview because they have not been taught the value of service to God and each other. There are many reasons for this, beginning with the mindset that God's will, sovereignty, purpose, and plans are somehow negotiable. The Bible says to train a child in the way he should go (Proverbs 22:6). As parents and the church, we have failed to train our younger generation on what is truly important because we have not lived a life that reflects our professed beliefs.

If taught when a child is young, the Bible teaches basic principles to set a biblical foundation for success in their walk of faith. Jesus said, "Feed my lambs, feed my sheep, and again feed my sheep," while preparing Peter for his upcoming assignment (John 21:15-17). Lambs represent the children of God, unlearned and in need of guidance, direction, and protection. The first sheep represents those who know the Lord and follow Him. The last sheep represents the mature believer who can teach and be accountable to God. As a parent, you are responsible for establishing your values in your home and with your family. Start with fundamental values, then expound upon and add to them regularly. Below is a sample of how you can set up values in your home. This list is not exhaustive, and you can make your own. The goal is to teach children not about the imaginary Easter Bunny, Santa Claus, or the ghost and goblins of Halloween but about principles that reflect accountability and responsibility to God in Christ Jesus.

- Judge not, and you will not be judged, for, by the measure that you judge, it will be returned to you (Luke 6:37).

- Condemn not, and you will not be condemned (Luke 6:37).

- Forgive, and you shall be forgiven. For if you do not forgive others, your Father in heaven will not forgive you (Luke 6:37).

And why do you look at the speck in your brother's eye but do not consider the plank in your own eye? Or how can you say brother let me remove the speck from your eye and there is a plank is in your own eye? Hypocrite! First remove the plank from your own eye then you can see clearly to remove the speck from your brother's eye (Matthew 7:3-5).

Then He said to the disciples; "it is impossible that no offenses should come, but woe to him through whom they do come! It would be better for him if a millstone were hung around his neck and cast into the sea than he should offend one of these little ones (Luke 17:1-2).

• Death and life are in the power of the tongue (Proverbs 18:21).

• You will be justified, and by your words, you will be condemned (Matthew 12:37).

• Do not be deceived. God is not mocked; whatever a man sows that he will also reap. For he who sows to the flesh will of the flesh reap corruption, but he who sows to the Spirit will of the Spirit reap everlasting life (Galatians 6:7-9).

• If you confess with your mouth the Lord Jesus and believe in your heart that God has raised Him from the dead, you will be saved. For with the heart, one believes unto righteousness, and with the mouth, confession is made unto salvation (Romans 10: 9-10).

• You will know my disciples by their love (John 13:35).

Love your Lord your God with all your heart, all your mind, all your soul, and all your strength, and love your neighbor as yourself (Mark 12:30-31).

Seek first the Kingdom of God, and its righteousness in all of these things will be added unto you (Matthew 6:33). For God so loved the world that He gave His only begotten Son, that whosoever believes in Him shall not perish but have everlasting life (John 3:16).

- Not everyone who says to me, "Lord, Lord," shall enter the Kingdom of heaven but only those who do the will of my Father in heaven (Matthew 7:21).

- As I live, says the Lord, every knee shall bow, and every tongue shall confess to God (Romans 14:11).

- Worship the Lord your God and Him only you shall serve (Matthew 4:10)

- Be Holy for I am Holy (Leviticus 11:44)

- And He said to man, "Behold the fear of the Lord, that is wisdom, and to turn away from evil is understanding," (Job 28:28).

The Third Expose: Church Legitimacy Testing

There are five criteria of the Christian walk that the Lord will judge His Church on for successful inheritance of the rewards He has set before those who love Him and obey His commands. The Bible says I know your works, love, service, faith, and patience (Revelation 2:19), these five attributes the Lord identified in His Churches as acceptable or unacceptable for legitimacy in his Kingdom.

1.) Works. Your work (fruit) is the evidence of your faith

(James 2:18). Everyone's work will be reviewed over the entirety of your time on earth and written in the Books as evidence and a witness of your belief and trust in God through Christ Jesus and the power of the Holy Spirit that works and lives inside every True Believer. "This evidence is divided into three areas of how you lived your life on this earth: toward God, others, and within yourself," (Mark 12:33).

A. Toward God

• Love (faithfulness to God in Christ Jesus by the power of the Holy Spirit.)

• Peace (Of God, With God, and In God.) (OWI)

• Joy (The joy of the Lord supersedes the temporary and fluctuating happiness this world offers.)

B. Toward your brother, sister, neighbor, friend, and enemy

• Kindness

• Goodness

• Patience

C. Exhibited in Your Inner Being

• Meekness (In your Spirit)

• Faithfulness (In your soul)

• Self-Control (In and with your body)

2.) "Love your Lord your God with all your heart, mind, strength, and soul," (Mark 12:29-32). Love is the motivation behind all God does and what we do as His children that bear His image. The Bible says to do all things in love (1 Corinthians 16:14).

3.) Service. Your service involves three areas of commitment to the Lord:

• Offering your body as a living sacrifice

• Living Holy

• Being acceptable in the sight of God (Romans 12:12)

4.) Faith. Without faith, it is impossible to please God. For a man must believe God exists and that he is a rewarder of those who faithfully trust in Him (Hebrews 11:6). Faith is the foundation and hope of the True Believer that God is and will do what He says He will do. You are not saved by the work you do; Your works are evidence of the amount of faith in the promises of God you have. Salvation is achieved only by faith through grace (Ephesians 2:8).

5.) Patience. During the tribulation period, the Lion of the Tribe of Judah described the patience of the Saints; here are those who keep the commandments of God and the faith of Jesus (Revelation 14:12). One of the most deceptive concepts among the church today is that everybody will be saved. This doctrine is not biblical or true and is contrary to what the Bible teaches. While the world and the church focus primarily on quantity and how many people will be saved on the earth, God is more focused on quality. This concept can be backed up by scripture because it speaks of the remnant throughout the Holy Scriptures. The remnant is God's covenant to Israel that He would never wholly annihilate His chosen people. God is first Holy, set apart, and His children can be identified by the traits and characteristics they also share that reflect Jesus in them. However, people like to compare themselves with others unmistakably worse than themselves to gauge their salvation. Faith and belief in Christ Jesus negate that train of thought and set the playing field even so that no one can boast of their work compared to others. The standard God in Christ Jesus and the power of the Holy Spirit that works and lives inside every True Believer focuses on is quality, meaning holiness, not just quantity, as His priority. In Noah's days, only eight souls of the millions on the earth at that time repopulated the earth (The Bible Sojourner). Holiness, the church, and sanctification mean everything to God. God is Holy, and as His children, He requires us to be Holy, or we are illegitimate. The Bible states that many will perish because they refuse to repent (Revelation 9:20). These unrepentant individuals choose death and damnation as opposed to the life and peace offered to them at the confrontation with their eternity. God's holiness standard will never change, and all in Christ Jesus are made clean. The question is, however, are you living a (Matthew 7:21) lifestyle in fear of the words "depart from me; I never knew you?" Even if you don't think this verse applies to you (which rarely, few ever do), this is why you need to get tested immediately!

The Fourth Expose: Did God say it?

The True Church and all the other false churches have a problem today as others in history have heard from the Lord and said what God has told them to say. The term "thus says the Lord" is spoken by everyone these days with a microphone or platform. They all proclaim through the utterance of the Holy Spirit, they receive their message, but this is not true. The Bible is clear that God does nothing without advising His prophets (Amos 3:7). Every day, you can hear from one pulpit to the next pulpit across the world the radical Revelation the Spirit assembly has revealed to all kinds of preachers and teachers who have never tested for the Holy Spirit. Just about everything, even fundamental Christian doctrine like sexual immorality, has found loopholes deemed acceptable in the church today. The more I began to write, the deeper the Spirit led me into my actual assignment.

I noticed that certain concepts the Lord placed in me to provoke me to ponder, study, and write in prison ministry strongly resembled the problems we face in the church today. My worldly, natural view of prison ministry did not come close to what the Spirit was preparing me for with this message that I deliver to the church of this present age. It was three years of preparation before I made the connection after ministering to a demographic of people that included the naturally and physically incarcerated, the previously incarcerated, the disabled veteran, the poor, the homeless, and people of a wayward lifestyle. So, I asked the Lord about whom these books were written and inquired if these books were to fix the church. I was caught off guard because after being a victim and experiencing church hurt from the last two churches I served, I was the last person wanting to go back to the church after being pulled out.

The Fifth Expose: Seven Churches

The Spirit said three things to me I want to share with you about the condition of the church in the 21st century. The first thing the Spirit said to me was, "There is nothing wrong with the Church." Jesus is the Head of the church, and as He is perfect and blameless, so is the church in which He established acceptable unto God and by the power of His Holy Spirit." As it has been with churches throughout history,

283

the problem with the present church is summed up as a matter of heart disease. The motives, intentions, and opportunities of the leaders who profess to know, commune, and relay the will of God, have drastically broken down. Further, the spiritual eyes and ears of the church body are increasingly subjected and being replaced by temporary and fleeting worldly desires and possessions.

The Spirit asked me the second question: "Which church are you talking about?" The Spirit identified seven spirits found in the seven churches our Lord and Savior mentions in Revelation Chapters Two and Three. They are as follows:

- The False Teaching Church does not teach the Word of God.

- False Prophesying Church does not know the will of God.

- The Dead Church has no spiritual discernment.

- The Unrepentant Church refuses to confess their sins.

- The Lukewarm Church refuses to choose service to God or the world.

- The Backsliding Church is filled with repeat offenders of the known will of God.

- The Overcoming Church, referred to as the "True Church," is the only Church Christ Jesus created and is coming back to retrieve.

The True Church is the body of Christ, meaning "His called out people," where God desires His temple to be located (1 Corinthians 3:16-17). This church consists of many people making up one body of True Believers functioning in the same mindset, work, and goals; to further the message of the Kingdom of God to an unbelieving world.

All seven types of churches, individual and collective as a group, exhibit conditions (C4) and operate in dispositions (D5) in their hearts that require daily testing in their work, patience, love, faith, and service to Christ Jesus. No one participates in this walk of faith untainted from the enemies' pressures, deception, and temptations. The Word of God is proven, tested, and tried to deliver all who trust and believe unto righteousness (Proverbs 30:5-7).

The third thing the Spirit said to me regarding the condition of today's church is that the church is not the problem. Christ Jesus built the "True Church," and the church is perfect. It is, as we discussed in Chapter Six, "That Thing Before the Church," causing all the division, strife, and condescension. The church has been infiltrated by what Apostle Paul identified in the early church of Corinth as sectarianism (1

Corinthians 3:4). Church members began focusing on the person who delivered the word instead of the "Word" Himself. This topic, discussed in Chapter Six, concerning the inability of the churches to be on one accord, identified the different types of denominations, varying doctrines, and religious traditions that plague the twenty-first-century church.

The solution for church legitimacy, bringing all churches under the umbrella of the True Church, rests in the willingness of people to acknowledge and accept the work of the Holy Spirit.

There is no church legitimacy without the presence of the Holy Spirit that guides the believer in these nine areas of their Christian daily walk: love, peace, and joy toward God, kindness, goodness, forgiveness toward your brother, and a sincere attribution of faithfulness, humility, and self-control in your demeanor.

The Sixth Expose: Where do you think you are going with that?

Blindly consumed with hate, oppression, persecution of nations, and their skewed philosophy of what and who is right and good, this country and the world are perishing. People in authority prioritize mercy and justice based on personal agendas, racial and ethnic bias. Yes, we should be concerned. We should be very concerned because this world and everything in it could all be over in a second. At the rate at which we are heading, people's natural heart condition will write them an eternal ticket they cannot repay. Do you know, as we speak, there is a nuclear arms race brewing again?

The world's condition is not going to improve, and this country and the hundred and ninety-four like it are in dire straits, meaning the shaking of all things is happening right before our eyes (Haggai 2:6-7). The good news for those who reside in the legitimate church is that your salvation is nearer today than yesterday! The rest of the churches and the world, however, if something doesn't change soon to ignite a revival of repentance in their hearts, people will perish. Many of which you may be related to or know personally.

This synopsis is not my opinion, and it's not just my interpretation; it's the Word of God. Everyone who has ever lived on this earth will go before the Lord for judgment one day. This day of judgment will consist of a life review of the five critical areas of evidence of your belief in Christ Jesus as Lord (Master, servant) and Savior (substitution, propitiation for your sins), the judge for what you have done in this body on the earth. The Bible says for we must all appear before the Judgment seat of Christ that each one may receive the things done in the body, according to what he has done, whether good or bad (2 Corinthians 5:10). Our Lord and Savior Christ Jesus further elaborated on the determining factors for believers when considered for entrance into the Kingdom of God and heaven. Patience, endurance, and love are traits of the True Church and evidence of our faith, works, and service to the Lord in this body in our time on this earth.

Charity (Love) "Love the Lord your God with all your heart, mind, soul, and strength," (Mark 12:30-31). You will know my disciples by their love, (John 13:35). Love covers a multitude of sins, (1 Peter 4:8). And now, these three remain faith, hope, and love, but the greatest of these is love, (1 Corinthians 13:13).

Faith. Hebrews 11:6, "but without faith, it is impossible to please Him for he who comes to God must believe that He is a rewarder of them who diligently seek him."

Works. Your works do not save you, for salvation is by grace alone (Ephesians 2:8-9), but the flip side of that same coin is at the judgment seat of Christ, you will be accountable for your works in the body (John 5:28-29). The Bible says, "and I saw the dead, small and great stand before God and the books were open, and another book was opened which is The Book of Life and the dead were judged out of those things which were written in the books according to their works," (Revelation 20:12).

Service. I beseech you, therefore, brethren, by the mercies of God, that you present your bodies a living sacrifice, holy, acceptable to God, which is your reasonable service. And do not be conformed to this world, but be transformed by the renewing of your mind, that you may prove what is that good and acceptable and perfect will of God (Romans 12:1-2).

Patience *the Lord is not slack concerning his promise as some count slackness but is long-suffering toward us, not willing that any should perish, but that should all come to repentance* (2 Peter 3:9).

Envision the Promise: Do you not know that you are the temple of God and that the Spirit of God dwells in you? If anyone defiles the temple of God, God will destroy him. For the temple of God is holy, which temple you are (1 Corinthians 3:16-17).

Chapter Fourteen
I SENT IT: CHECK IT MATE

"But when ye shall hear of wars and commotions, be not terrified: for these things must first come to pass; but the end is not by and by," (Luke 21:9). "For this is what the Sovereign Lord says: How much worse will it be when I send against Jerusalem my four dreadful judgments— sword and famine and wild beasts and plague—to kill its men and their animals," (Ezekiel 14:21). "And now I have told you before it comes, that when it does come to pass, you may believe," (John 14:29).

The First Expose: Chess The chess game is a highly intellectual game between two opposing Kings and their servants on a sixty-four-square playing board, representing their Kingdoms. The game's objective is to seize the other person's king by infiltrating his Kingdom and subduing his resources which enshrines the lone-standing king as victorious and ruler over both Kingdoms. The game involves a high degree of cognitive ability, fluid intelligence, and planning. As it is in the natural, so it is in the spiritual (McClure). The chess game of eternal life has two opposing sides: 1.) the Kingdom of Light, ruled by God, by the power of His Holy Spirit, and His commander in Chief, Christ Jesus. Jesus has His subjects, the church made up of believers and His Angels, that stand by His side for this battle of literally the dominion of heaven and earth for eternity. The opposing player is 2.) the Kingdom of darkness ruled by the outcast Satan. He also has subjects: the fallen angels, unbelievers of this world, and two unknown players from the earth realm, soon revealed as the false prophet and the beast consisting of corrupt government leaders who will deceive the entire world (Revelation 12:9). The board or Kingdom where these two teams will fight this final battle is called Armageddon, and this is where all Kingdoms will become one Kingdom of Heaven and Earth under Christ Jesus (Revelation 21:1). This prophecy was strategic and intentional, given seven hundred years before by the prophet Isaiah. The prediction stated Jesus was to make his appearance as Immanuel, meaning, "God with us." He would be the Savior of all humankind, the Prince of Righteousness and Peace, and the only name by which all men would be saved. Two thousand years later, precisely as outlined in the prophetic writings, everything is happening right according to schedule. As written, we find ourselves in a worse predicament than at first as this world, earth, and the evil one that has now received judgment and condemnation get more anxious because of the inevitable outcome. The First Coming, the Lamb of God, the One who sits at the Father's right hand, patiently awaits His new duty and assignment as *Judge*.

The Second Expose: Ultimate Strategy

Contrary to popular beliefs, some can't see the hand of God in and on all things because they are not aware of what the primary will of our God is for His people's future and this present earth. It is not to entirely save this physical world but to prepare whosoever wills in it for rights and access to live in the perfect world to come (Revelation 21:7). The Holy Scriptures repeatedly tell us the outcome of this world and not in parable form as other prophecies. This world's demise is fire. Two types: spiritual, judgment, and literal, which is fervent heat (Jeremiah 7:20). Only those unbelievers, those who live in delusions, or those blinded by the truth of God expect any different outcome besides what the Bible explicitly states. Just like in the days of old, because it hasn't happened yet, those people live in vain and futility.

One of my favorite teachers and pastors, Dr. Dharius Daniels, says it like this, "When God is doing something, He is doing something for your intended good, and when He is doing nothing, He is still doing something; blessed be the hand of the Lord! "The point of the matter is if He is doing something, it is for your good and a specific reason, and if He is doing nothing, it is still for your interest and a particular purpose! In this new world to come, the Bible says the new Jerusalem is coming down out of the sky, and God has achieved exactly what He purposed all along. He vowed from the beginning that He would have a people of His very own, one where He will be our God, and we will be His people (Exodus 6:7). Everything manifested for six thousand plus years, to this very day, is a means to an ultimate strategic plan that brings one domain to an end and another Kingdom to the beginning of rulership for eternity.

The Third Expose: No Rest for the Wicked

"Say to the righteous that it shall be well with them, for they shall eat the fruit of their doings. Woe to the wicked! It shall be ill with him," for the reward of his hands shall be given him (Isaiah 3:10-11). This battle for eternity has already been won from the foundations of the world. Everything was put in its proper place by God. The devil and his demons already know it, the True Church is reminded of it, and if many who are still on the fence would read their Bibles and seek the Holy Spirit in these last days, they would sincerely realize it too. Satan's permanent abode (SPA) has already been set up, awaiting their eternal guest to come in the order of their prescribed mark of condemnation (Jude 1:6) (Revelation 20:10, 14-15).

If individuals living in these last days understood what the hand of the Lord looks like on a person condemned to death because of what is written in their books, some would think twice before making short-term choices that have eternal consequences. Suicides, murder, oppression, fornicators, and every ungodly thing that has ever existed have their place in God's plan; "There is no peace," says my God, "For the wicked," (Isaiah 57:27). This generation of wicked people who believe God does not see them, or that He doesn't care are sadly mistaken (Malachi 2:17). This generation who lives any way they like, then hope vainly they die to nothingness; like they were never here, have a rude awakening of torment and regret in store for their immediate future by the Messenger of the covenant (Malachi 3:2-3).

In this season, we endure despite all the life-changing events we have been through as the church reflects on the wake-up call we received in 2020 and into 2021, yet some still reject Jesus. Many want a piece of Jesus (minus denying oneself, discipleship, and bearing their cross). Some have built their own Jesus out of the deception and imaginations of their own heart, denying the holiness God in Christ Jesus requires (1 Peter 1:15-17). The outlook is grim, and the prognosis is we have work to do and not a lot of time left to do it, for we are closer today than we were yesterday to the return of our Lord and Savior (Romans 13:11). There is no going back to normal. The days when God could overlook man's evilness, wickedness, and lawlessness are almost over because the time of grace is all but over. No other time in history has humanity had the capability to destroy the earth at the touch of a button or decimate the entire planet out of greed, pride, and covetousness. All humankind has undergone Babylon 7 DEFCON II: The Rejection of "I Am Who I Am" for "AI" technology seeking Artificial Intelligence. No fear of God, a dulled heart, and spiritual death have sealed the doom for this generation who are not a part of the True Church. Where much is given, much is required, and no generation has had greater access to truth than this current generation. Men blatantly deny His existence and sovereignty in a world where everything points back to God, the creator. However, the children of God have been sealed unto redemption by His Holy Spirit (Ephesians 4:30).

The Fourth Expose: Checkmate

Checkmate is a statement given to the opposing player in the chess game when he has successfully maneuvered his assets by a predetermined set of rules to entrap the opponent. Check warns that the next move results in subduing and capturing the opponent's most valuable asset, his king. The game concludes when one player is ultimately victorious because his assets are the only ones left, or the other king just has no move to make. Chess is a complex game filled with special favor for specific pieces that allow them greater flexibility over less important but valuable pieces. The most powerful asset an opponent has is its king. All the other components are subordinate and designed to protect the king at any cost, even incarceration themselves. If the king becomes subdued at any point in the game, the game is immediately over. This move is called "checkmate." Likewise, in the Kingdom of Heaven, these last days are like the checkmate position where darkness knows it is but a matter of time but with eternal consequences. Jesus the Christ is our eternal King, and He will conquer all the kings of the earth (Revelation 20:4). Until Christ returns, He has left His Church to be His body, hands, feet, and mouth, to be an example and proclaim to the world His imminent return. He has left leaders in His Church to feed His flock He calls His sheep, with knowledge and instruction in preparation for things that must transpire before His return. He has also not left us unprepared, but He has given us a checklist of things we can expect to occur. This checklist outlines specific cultural events, natural phenomena, disasters, trials, tribulations, and hardships that require our patience, perseverance, and endurance (PPE) to enter the upcoming Kingdom of Heaven here on earth. Here are ten individual scriptures referencing things that must occur in the last days as written in the Holy Scriptures. These events must happen first, but these things are just the beginning of many sorrows to come (Matthew 24:8).

- False Christ (Matthew 24:4-5)

- Wars and rumors of wars (Matthew 24:6)

- Nation against nations and Kingdoms against Kingdoms (Matthew 24:7-8)

- Christians not enduring sound doctrine (2 Timothy 4:1-5)

- Scoffers who deny the imminent return of our Lord and Savior Christ Jesus (2 Peter 3:3)

- False proclamations of peace and safety (1 Thessalonians 5:3)

- Men walking after their lusts (Jude 1:16)

- Men heaping treasure for the last days (James 5:3)

- False preachers and false prophets (Matthew 24:11)

- Increase in knowledge and travel (Daniel 12:4)

Unlike the game of chess, there is no stalemate. From the foundations of this earth, prophesied thousands of years ago, a Winner was declared, an Overcomer, One who will inherit all things, inhabit the earth, and rule it with a rod of iron forever (Revelation 2:27).

Only a few pastors, preachers, ministers, teachers, and evangelists are bold enough or will put themselves out there on a Holy Spirit-inspired olive branch to warn, advise, and prepare this generation's church for the desperate condition we are experiencing today. This generation is mostly fed on feel-good, make me happy sermons of the blessings of God as opposed to what is happening to this world in real-time, right before our very eyes. Sometimes, silence is a good thing for some teachers, biblically speaking, because if God did not tell you to say it, you better not. Though it works both ways, if the Lord sends a specific message through you to share, then you must share it. The flip side of that coin is if you are a shepherd in charge of a flock and not in tune with exactly what God is doing in this season, how can you effectively equip the saints? Moreover, how can you ensure that the body of Christ is knowledgeable and prepared for the spiritual warfare prophesied and now sits on the horizon, literally sitting on our front porches, not knocking but beating the door down to consume the unprepared?

The church's inability to discern the acceptable or unacceptable state of current affairs contaminating fundamental biblical doctrine is sending up serious red flags about the church's preparedness headed into these last days.

The declining growth and severity of the delusions people of the church are experiencing regarding amoral and sexual behavior signal a severe case of heart disease.

The enemies of Christ Jesus are exposed, and without a doubt, this nation in which we live is under judgment. All the players except for two are either in or moving toward their prescribed places. The True Church and those who profess their allegiance in word, deed, or pretense have much to do. By the word of their testimony, the blood of the lamb, and they that do not love their lives to the death, this is the patience of the overcoming church (Revelation 12:11).

There is a shortage of salt and light (Matthew 5:13-16); the examples Christ Jesus left for this age to influence and guide the church through the global outburst of rebellion and denial He predicted. The purpose of being the salt and light of the earth is to reflect good works, thereby glorifying our Father in heaven. Increasingly more individuals who profess to know Christ and claim salvation by His innocent blood are poor salt and light examples because they are spiritually dead or hidden like the servant with the one talent (Matthew 25:14-30).

"The Lord said to my Lord, 'Sit at my right hand Till I make your enemies your footstool,'" (Psalms 110:1). The lack of salt and light to influence and guide God's children in Christ Jesus in this global outburst of rebellion and denial is hindered by the same individuals who claim to know Christ and are saved by His innocent blood. The problem is, which has been said repeatedly, people don't believe God is in control, and He is who He says he is. Period. God has a flip side phrase that He frequently uses, especially in the books of Ezekiel (Ezekiel 6:10). Repeated forty-two times, this phrase, **"*Then you shall know I am the Lord,*"** always comes as a precursor and warning of future consequential events brought about by man's refusal to acknowledge God's right hand (Nelson, Thomas).

In 2016, when the former President first came into power, I sought the Lord about what was happening. I know the Bible says God appoints kings (Daniel 2:21), and Christ Jesus said to Pilate you would be able to do nothing unless My Father granted this to you from above (John 19:11). I didn't understand then that regardless of what it looked like, if this man was in power, God alone put him there for His purposes and not for our approval, comfort, or immediate understanding. We sometimes don't understand as the church; we could be fighting not for God's will but against God's will because of our human understanding and feelings. There is a set date and time, and you must understand that God will get enough of this mess in the hearts of man (Revelation 10:6). The True Church Jesus built isn't growing the way He instructed his followers in his word. Many have put the carriage in front of the horse seeking unconditional love and eternal life without a commitment to service or covenant of faith. Still, he was never caught off guard, addressing this problem beforehand. In Revelation, chapters two and three, Jesus outlines and tells us what to fix to get back into the alignment of the Holy Spirit in us, the church in Him, all unto God as acceptable.

The Fifth Expose: The Shaking

As in the earlier days when humankind refused to know God, believe God, and repent of their wicked ways, the Lord said once again; I will shake all things, (Hebrews 12:26). The shaking refers to everything connected to the Kingdoms of this world (human, natural, animal, and demonic) that are not proceeding into the next world acceptable to God (2 Peter 3:10). This advent is the precursor to the end of all things as we know it for this age. The source is not a man-ordained or controlled event, though he plays an intricate part in the destruction of this world. God alone allowed humanity to follow their wicked ways to their doom but prepared a way out for those who trust and believe in Him through His Son, Christ Jesus. God allowed the consequences built into His laws, called curses, to overtake and make His word faithful, but humanity failed to heed the instruction, even after two thousand years of warnings. The shaking includes heaven, earth, sea, dry land, and the nations. This shaking has already begun and surely has picked up the pace. God has shut down the manufactured buildings made of metal. mortar, brick, sand, wood, and glass in these last days to open the doors of the church of your heart in hopes of a life-altering relationship with you. What God, through Christ Jesus, and the power of the Holy Spirit, encourages you to do in this season is to seek Him by picking up and reading your basic instructions before leaving earth (Bible). God's children are blood-washed heirs (first to the Jew) or adopted, regenerated Gentiles who have accepted Christ Jesus as their personal Savior through grace by faith alone, not by anything they have done or will do but totally by our faith. The Bible says, "Ask, and it will be given to you, knock, and it will be opened for you, and seek and you will find," (Matthew 7:7). This doctrine is outstanding, preaching very encouraging, yet very few see the flip side to this point that this promise is only to the children of God. It is not to people who are not legitimately a part of the fold. My friend, the reality is that everyone on the earth is God's creation, but God does not consider everyone His child. I am a recruiter for the Kingdom of God, and our God is good, gracious, and excellent in all His ways, statutes, and precepts.

Envision the Promise: The righteous perishes, and no man takes it to heart; Merciful men are taken away, while no one considers that the righteous is taken away from evil. He shall enter into peace; They shall rest in their beds, each walking in his uprightness *(Isaiah 57:1-2)*.

Chapter Fifteen

THE TRANSITION FROM WILL TO SHALL

"If you confess with your mouth the Lord Jesus and believe in your heart that God has raised Him from the dead, you will be saved," (Romans 10:9-25) "Jesus said to her, "I am the resurrection and the life. He who believes in Me, though he may die, he shall live. 26 And whoever lives and believes in Me shall never die. Do you believe this?" (John 11:25-26). For yet a little while, and he that shall come will come, and will not tarry," (Hebrews 10:37).

The First Expose: Will Live

The most deceptive trick the enemy has employed on this generation is fear that you will die. The truth is that everything dies, and we learn this early on in our short lives. However, this death issue is not the end for you or your most significant problem to date. Right in line with the enemy's bag of tricks and a playbook of half-truths and lies, the truth is that you will live somewhere after your EARTH suit expires. The term "will live" describes the future of everyone who has ever lived on this earth. Everyone will face judgment, the dead unbeliever, the dead in Christ Jesus, and those still living on this earth when Christ returns. It boils down to this; God already knows your expected end. Your job is to faithfully secure your name in the Book of Life, written before the foundations of the world. Faithfulness and obedience to God are how you will avoid the second death, which is separation from God for eternity in hell. The enemy would have you believe everything contrary to the truth of the holiness of God. The enemy is already defeated. His only mission now is to take as many with him as possible in his time left. Many will gamble with their salvation only to realize the truth too late will be an eternal price.

When I received the word in my spirit early on Tuesday morning, March 7, 2017, that I Will Live & Not Die, the bleeding I endured for eighteen-plus years prior didn't stop that day. My cholesterol and blood pressure didn't magically disappear overnight. My C.O.P.D., sarcoidosis, rheumatoid arthritis, and the traumatic depression I had endured for numerous years didn't disappear right upon the confession of my belief. However, what did happen early that Tuesday morning was I made up my mind and believed the Word of God that was placed in my spirit and soul, that if I confessed my sins, He would save me. What I also believed then in my heart, and now continue to witness through this written work, is the confidence God was and still is in total control, and his

Right Hand (Psalms 139:17) is upon me to proclaim His good works in my life.

Believing in my heart set the tone that motivated me to spend eternity with Jesus in the land of the living because I did not want to die. My intentions have been tested repeatedly over the years, and by the mercy and grace of God, when I so often miss the mark, He still makes ways out of no way. Wrestling daily with the things of this world, the accuser, and just as deceptive my flesh nature, I consciously take every opportunity to worship, praise, serve, and glorify my Lord and Savior with all my heart and mind, strength, and soul. It was clear as day and evident as I recounted all the grace and mercy I have received in my life, and I finally realized that God had a plan and purpose for me from the beginning. Did I have any idea of the journey God would send me on? No, I literally would have self-sabotaged myself before His divine plans for the rest of my life ever had a chance to catch root. Knowing what I know now, it would have been too surreal for me. This current version of me was not birthed by my mother, my pastor, or anything I could do myself, but only by God's grace, mercy, and love in my daily life through Christ Jesus. The Christ Jesus who loved me and saved me by the power of The Holy Spirit that sealed me unto redemption.

The Second Expose: It's Not What You Think

All humanity knows of God, but very few truly know God. It's like having a favorite athlete or celebrity figure. In this age of social media, you know everything about their lives, such as where they live, their relationships, family, and whatever else they want to reveal. The issue is that you don't know them because they don't know you. They don't call you and see how you are doing or invite you over for dinner or vice versa because you don't know each other. Likewise, truly knowing God is the problem with many professed Christians today. They claim to know God, but God does not know them. Scripture corroborates this truth from the Father and Son's recorded admission. The Father said, "My people are fools; they do not know me responding to their constant rebellion and disobedience since leaving Egyptian captivity. They are skilled at doing evil and knowing, not how to do good," (Jeremiah 4:22). In another biblical reference, God identifies the problem, citing their lack of mercy, no regard for the truth, and refusal to know His ways (Hosea 4:3). Jesus also called it just like it was, telling the people, "The Father honors me whom you say is your God, yet you have not known Him, but I know Him and am from Him," (John 8:55). As expressed repeatedly in this book, we are only here by God's grace and mercy. No one deserves eternal life because all have sinned, and the punishment for sin is death (Romans 6:23). Knowing God means you understand that this life is not about you. This life and eternity that follows it includes you but is not about your will but the will of God. Christ Jesus said if you try to save this life, you will lose it, but you will gain it if you lose this life for My sake (Luke 9:24). Boom! That one verse blew three-quarters of the theology of this current generation.

Peanut butter and jelly sandwich Christian-minded individuals know the verse and quote the scriptures but rarely produce the fruit of the word in their lives. The word that would otherwise create life-altering change and power too often is disregarded and ignored in their everyday Christian walk of faith. The saddest thing these people refuse to realize about this short life isn't that they will die but that they will live and face judgment one day. Pride is the pompous attitude that infuriates the only true Righteous and Sovereign God more than anything. This attitude mimics the adversary, Satan, the enemy of God who has already received judgment (John 16:24).

On April 19, 2011, while at the crossroads of life, halfdead, full of remorse and personal failures, I knew a choice was necessary regarding my future. I could shrug off this incident, play the victim, as I had done multiple times before, or change. This decision is the very thing that I now witness to others so boldly and passionately. A Good Man Is Hard to Find: Adam Where Are You, the book by Reverend Dr. Michael L. Henderson, outlines biblical steps to becoming a good man in a world where good men are scarce. My thoughts and intentions were to clean myself up and live my life as a God-fearing believer. You see, when the Lord told me I would live and not die, I had no idea that wasn't a good thing at the time! Even though He also said He didn't heal me for me, I still didn't quite catch on. I was simply happy as many are ignorantly walking around daily in my sins, transgressions, and iniquities, sitting up in church, dropping a few dollars off now and then, not knowing I wasn't anywhere near "there" yet. God had a plan for me that involved patience, endurance, and perseverance on a level I would never have imagined in five lifetimes.

What I would soon find out is God means every word He says. Period. One would be in awe of the numerous times I changed the title of this book, always reverting to the original title because I didn't understand it was God's book, not mine. I wasn't reading the Bible and writing relevant stories. I was writing through the Holy Spirit, and the Bible corroborated everything I was writing.

I noticed I first entitled the book *You Will Live & Not Die:*

Forced Hand, but in later revisions, I also wrote *You Shall Live & Not Die: Forced Hand*. So, which was it, and what was the difference between "will and shall?" What the Spirit revealed to me for this good work is "will live" speaks to every human being that has ever lived without exception. "Shall live," on the other hand, is restricted to the children of God, given to Christ Jesus, before the foundations of the world. Once I grasped this concept, I understood why I must write as led in the Spirit. This experience later prepared me to write boldly the things I see, unafraid of how this book is perceived in the world but always giving the truth in love and faithfulness. It was necessary that I annotated *will* and *shall* through the Spirit because this opportunity built my faith and confidence that I heard correctly from the Lord. They were correct for this good work and a steppingstone for my future work.

The Third Expose: The Books

According to the Holy Scriptures, there are at least three complete sets of books in heaven. The first is the Book of Life, which contains the names of every person who has ever lived and attained eternal life. The Book of Life is separate from the other books and contains only one thing; those who have received salvation through the blood of the Lamb and the word of their testimony (Revelation 12:11). Congratulations! If your name is in this book, you have officially transitioned from will live to shall live, and you have made it through the pearly gates of heaven (Revelation 21:21). The Book of Life has the names of all the redeemed of Christ Jesus and will live life eternally (Revelation 20:12). Again, not having your name written in the Book of Life means you have suffered condemnation. We must deal with the truth. Everyone will go to only one of two places, and you must choose! The Bible says everyone will be judged and given their just reward for their life on this earth and what they have done in this earthly body, either good or evil (2 Corinthians 5:10).

Everyone has a book in heaven with their name on it; what's in yours? Like it or not, everyone will discover the answer to that question at the marriage supper of the Lamb, the first resurrection, or the Great White Throne Judgment. The marriage supper of the Lamb is what I perceive as the rapture of the saints. There are many theories, and I am not here to argue; I write what I see. Regardless of the time or sequence of events, all three are described in the Holy Scriptures in detail. The first resurrection is only for True Believers who have endured during the tribulation, keeping God's commands and the testimony of Christ Jesus. The White Throne Judgement, the second death, is the resurrection for everyone after the one-thousand-year reign of Christ Jesus.

This final judgment has no power over the saved saints, prophets, and servants of Christ Jesus who participated in the first resurrection. The Bible says every man, on resurrection day, is raised from the first death, which is the expiration of these EARTH suits, to face sure judgment. This resurrection includes everyone who has ever lived. But everyone doesn't go to the same place.

The Bible says those who have done good in the body will rise to live life eternal with Jesus where He is. However, those who have done evil will rise to condemnation. There is no negotiation or mistake of someone ending up in heaven when they should have gone to the S.P.A. and vice versa. A completely accurate accounting of everyone's life is in heaven's books. The Book of Revelation, according to John, describes the second resurrection like this: "Then I saw a great white throne and Him who sat on it, from whose face the earth and the heaven fled away. And there was found no place for them. And I saw the dead, small and great, standing before God, and books were opened. And another book was opened, which is the Book of Life. And the dead were judged according to their works, by the things which were written in the books. The sea gave up the dead who were in it, and Death and Hades delivered up the dead who were in them.

And they were judged, each one according to his works. Then Death and Hades were cast into the lake of fire. This is the second death. And anyone not found written in the Book of Life was cast into the lake of fire," (Revelation 20:12-15).

The second book is the Little Book or The Book of Truth, known to us as the Bible or the Holy Scriptures (Revelation 10:10). The Holy Scriptures say, **He had a Little Book open in his hand. And he set his right foot on the sea and his left foot on the land** (Revelation 10:2). The feet of the angel placed on the land and the sea symbolize the earth's judgment. The command of God to Christ Jesus after His time on earth as the "Lamb of God" was to sit at His right hand until I make Your enemies Your footstool," (Hebrew 1:13). The Holy Bible is the most important book of your life because it alone contains the keys to life eternal. Basic Instructions Before Leaving Earth (Bible), an acronym often used to describe the Little Book, would mean more to people if they believed and understood its eternal importance. Everything you have read in this book is found in the Holy Scriptures, for they contain the Word of God, which is the Truth. The Book of Truth is used on earth "BEFORE" you die and get to heaven to lead you into all righteousness so you can avoid judgment and condemnation. The Holy Scriptures are suitable for: Instruction, Rebuking, Reproofing,

Correction, Godliness, Holiness, and Righteousness (2 Timothy 3:16-17).

The third of the three books is "Your Book." As the event described in the Holy Scriptures stated, **I saw the dead small and great standing before God, and "the books were opened."** One of those books, my friend, will be Your Book. It is written that every man will face judgment, not collectively, individually, being responsible for only himself (Romans 14:11). Your book will cover the five areas we mentioned in detail in Chapter Thirteen:

1.) Work

2.) Service

3.) Love

4.) Faith

5.) Patience

Our Lord and Savior advised the seven churches about these five areas of interest (Revelation 2:19) and went as far as blotting individuals out of His Book of Life for noncompliance. There may be many volumes (Hebrews 10:7) in your story, but only three points of interest will ultimately decide your fate; 1) your confession of faith and belief in Christ Jesus alone as Lord and Savior (John 3:18), 2) what God called you to do in Christ Jesus and by the power of the

Holy Spirit (Matthew 25:14-30) and 3) what you *actually* did in the body according to what is written in Your Book (Revelation 20:13, John 5: 28-29). "*Actually*" is purposely placed in italics here because many in this day and age remain deceived that somehow God does not know what each individual's heart (motivations, intentions, and opportunities) truly reflects in the relationship of being a member of His enduring church.

A good habit True Believers should remember daily is that a book with your name on it has already been written in eternity, and your life in this EARTH will dictate what's inside. The Bible says before the foundations of the world, "Our books were already fashioned for us," (Psalms 139:18). In another place, one translation says, "I know the plans I have for you, plans to prosper, and not harm you, plans of hope and future," (Jeremiah 29:11 NIV). As discussed in detail in Chapter One, there is an entity called time. I am not trying to explain or slightly understand how everything future, or past is in the present to God, but it is! What is biblically certain, however, remains while you are still on earth, still breathing, and having the opportunity to receive the word of the Lord; your book is being edited daily to reflect your life values and beliefs. The Bible says do not be deceived; whatever a man sows, he shall reap (Galatians 6:7-9).

Knowing what is pleasing and acceptable to God is a surefire way to avoid sin and therefore keep you and your book spotless for the day of Christ Jesus.

The Fourth Expose: The Kingdom of God Preached

The Holy Scriptures states, **"and this gospel of the Kingdom will be preached, in all the world as a witness to all the nations, and then the end will come" (Matthew 24:14).** The question many will ask about this book is why now and who are you? The answer to "why now" is unmistakably evident to anyone who has any knowledge of the Bible and lives in the twenty-first century. We covered the specifics of "why now" in Chapter Fourteen, *Check It Mate.* Who am I to carry such a world-changing word to the masses? Absolutely nobody but the least of His children saved by the cross, washed in the blood, partaking of His abundant grace and mercy. Why should you think that this word the good Lord placed in me is the valid message of the Kingdom? My answer is the same as anyone whom the Lord has called to do a good work. It has nothing to do with who I am but everything to do with God's will, in Christ Jesus, and by the power of His Holy Spirit. God's power is perfected in man's weaknesses, 2 Corinthians 12:9. At the beginning of this assignment, it was revealed to me, "I hid something in you where no one will find it." Now I understand, knowing that nothing of my own power and strength would have qualified me for this assignment but only the will, grace, and mercy of the Lord by his power alone.

Another one of my Peter experiences can explain why the Lord chose someone like me for this assignment. Apostle Peter, by all rights, could have been considered the least of the Apostles; one of the three, the closest of the twelve apostles and confessing till the death devotion only to deny his Lord and Savior three consecutive times. He was a self-professed sinner, asking the Lord Jesus to depart from him because of his shame. But to Peter's credit again, knowing the Lord when approached by Him, Peter did not refuse to follow the Lord. I have been on this journey to complete this good work for four years, stumbling often but never giving up on what I knew I was called to accomplish in the Kingdom. The Apostle Paul, however, is the best example. God was able to show His exceedingly steadfast mercy, abundant grace and unlimited power in a young man who was as far from the holiness God requires as you can get. In me the Lord can point to as an example that it is not always what you can't do but more so what people won't do because of what is in their heart.

The Lord did, however, prepare me as He did his servant Moses. The Bible says, and we know that all things work together for good to those who love God, to those who are the called according to *His* purpose. For whom He foreknew, He also predestined *to be* conformed to the image of His Son, that He might be the firstborn among many brethren. Moreover, whom He predestined, these He also called; whom He called, these He also justified; and whom He justified, these He also glorified (Romans 8:28-30).

Moses, a Hebrew raised in the house of the Egyptians, the same nation that persecuted his people for four hundred and thirty years. God planned this before the foundations of the world so that Moses would learn everything, he needed to accomplish his assignment from the people God would later judge. I likewise was educated in the vocation and discipline of Human Resources for twenty years, which has given me a unique perspective on service in the Kingdom of God. Human Resources is the backbone and framework of any organization. The company's ethics, integrity, mission, goals, and vision are entirely communicated and facilitated through the human resource department. Whether it's hiring, firing, compliance, training, and development, or the most crucial part to most people, their salary or wages, Human Resources is the department you go to see about it. Human Resources is the liaison between the C.E.O. of the company, the organization's department leaders, and the organization's most valuable asset, its employees. Wouldn't it be great in the same respect if the church had an independent entity whose job was to interpret company policy and then enforce compliance and accountability for department leaders and employees alike?

Working in Human Resources, you must perform duties that require you to hold people accountable for actions they are uncomfortable or unwilling to do. Disciplinary actions incurred because of employee misconduct, excessive tardiness, or engaging coworkers in ways that sexually or verbally harass others can affect one's employment status and livelihood. Human Resource personnel must understand the ramifications of the incidents and be prepared to initiate the corresponding disciplinary action according to the organization's policies, standards, and procedures. Understanding and interpreting the precepts and principles of the Kingdom for transformation and implementation through "the books" is my assignment. I do this in service to the Kingdom of God during this season of my life (Luke 18:29, 30).

The Fifth Expose: Come Out!

Today, we no longer have the luxury of time to listen and adhere to this unjust and ungodly world and its rhetoric. The philosophy and teaching of this world have modeled its father, Satan, who had no intention of following God because of his corrupt heart. As the True Church, we must come out from among them and be separate, witnessing to the masses about who and what we believe with our very lives.

The deity of Christ as the Son of God enables Jesus Christ and gives Him the authority to raise the dead. The Creator of the Son of Man performed flawlessly His purpose to live, teach, heal, forgive, and reconcile an underserving world back to its creator. As a result, He was chastised, forsaken, beaten, crucified, and murdered, while never murmuring or lifting a finger in retaliation. These selfless acts afforded Jesus alone beside the Father, all power in heaven and the earth to judge and sentence.

The Sixth Expose: There Is No Angle

There are no angles, loopholes, or education levels concerning the qualifications for acceptance in the Kingdom of God. The wisdom of God is impartial and without hypocrisy (James 3:17). You don't have to be a theologian or philosopher, and one doesn't have to know Arabic, Hebrew, or Greek. The Holy Scriptures say that the teaching of the word gives understanding that even the simple-minded person can understand (Psalms 119:130 NLT). In another scripture reference, the Apostle Paul explains that some may suffer deception from the enemy considering the simplicity found in Christ Jesus. False teachers preaching another Jesus, believers receiving another spirit, or accepting a different gospel not given initially all contribute to the perversion of the good news our Lord and Savior imparted to His followers (2 Corinthians 11:3-4).

This is not the first time or the last time a messenger will address this prevalent issue of separation and holiness, so some may reason and regard this message as redundancy (Matthew 23:34). There is a set time for revealing all things (Luke 12:2-3). This work has thoroughly defined and refined this message of the Kingdom of God and the Kingdom of Heaven. There is no debate except among the ungodly of the position of the True Church in these last days to test all things and keep what is good and to abstain of all forms of evil (1 Thessalonians 5:2122).

The evil and wickedness of this world have reached the heavens, ears, and sight of God. Daily reprehensible plans, schemes, and systems usher in the Antichrist, the false prophet, and the beast into a far too willing and accommodating world to receive them. Just as humanity has done throughout history and will continue to do, the world will reject the Two Witnesses of God, who will come and condemn this world and its ways (Revelation 11:7). The signs and wonders people are waiting for are already here, and they walk around with access to it in their pockets. The cellular phone reveals pertinent information, but a person must know what he is looking for to retrieve the data. This unsuspecting generation of individuals lost in the technological upheaval will continue to up the ante on an already depraved human mind. Whatever you think you see, these times are far worse than you can ever imagine. The time has come; the table is set, and evil has begun to make its last pitch before the prophesied ending. And this is the will of Him who sent Me, that everyone who sees the Son and believes in Him may have everlasting life; and I will raise him at the last day (John 6:39-40). Kingdom Recruiting in the 21st century is a God-ordained strategy to initiate a Ramer word and perspective to the children of God in a world where hope is depleted and sometimes non-existent in some people's hearts. What is extremely hard for some Christians to come to grips with is that everything serves God. The good, the bad, life, death, those who choose to believe, and His adversaries who choose His indignation all serve the purposes of God. Regardless of the circumstances, God will always receive His glory. Long before even the beginning of time, God's history is unblemished. Being who He says He is and doing what He says He will do; is the reason He is God all by Himself (Numbers 23:19). However, some Christians try to understand with their natural eyes how God allows the good and the bad to exist for His purposes and plans. This human logic is why many cling to futile thinking and frustration, confining God in a box of their limited understanding.

The Bible is clear, loving God means keeping his commandments (1 John 5:2), and our Lord and Savior says if you love me, keep my word (John 14:15). *Houston, we have a problem.* This current generation, especially in the United States, has conformed to a governmental, cultural setting and environment that promotes a Kingdom contrary to the Kingdom Christians pray to come. This form of government system is not the Bible's government in which we should pray. No wonder why the government took prayer out of schools. When they repeat their daily prayers, some people don't take to heart what they are praying, "Your Kingdom come. Your will be done on earth as it is in heaven Matthew 6:10)." People pray for the Kingdom of God and Heaven to come here on earth but live in a way displayed by their actions and mindsets that suggest they want a democratic lifestyle in heaven. Our Lord and Savior is the crowned and eternal King of this entire world who has the keys of death and the grave.

The Lord, our God, will remove all forms of government not aligned with the Kingdom of our Lord and His Christ. (Revelation 11:15). The Holy Scriptures says, **"The seventh** angel sounded; and there were great voices in heaven saying, the Kingdoms of this world have become the Kingdoms of our Lord and of His Christ; He shall reign forever and ever," (Revelation 11:15 MEV).

The problems that promote the biggest challenge for this generation are unbelief and their C4D5 Chronic Affliction. Unbelief from the viewpoint that people still don't believe God is who He says He is; secondly, the C4D5 Chronic Affliction of humankind causes conditions and creates a disposition that places some people in denial of whom they think or say and delusional of whom they indeed are. Whatever we do here on earth, we are required to do it to the glory of God (Colossians 3:23-24), but man's heart wants the credit for himself. As stated before, knowing who you are in your EARTH suit is the first step in preparing your heart for availability and service to Christ Jesus and a commitment to the Kingdom of God and Heaven.

The Seventh Expose: Are We There Yet? Really??

The numbers don't lie as some people tend to do about how they see the condition of the current church. My assignment is to write what I see. What I see in the twenty-first-century contemporary church is disheartening, demoralizing, and sobering. The most disheartening fact is trying to speak life and peace to spiritually dead people. This sensual and carnal generation only wants to be fed what feels good devoid of true repentance and holiness. I am demoralized concerning many Believers who are SI²C³K (Suffering Internal Iniquity from Compromised, Contaminated, and Corrupted Knowledge) in this church dispensation. These individuals still believe God does not know what is in their hearts and that their participation in church activities will alleviate their pending judgement. Finally, it is sobering to see professed Christians who have no idea they have a book in heaven and, much less, have no clue what is in it. This fact is evident by what comes out of the mouths and the behaviors of those who profess to belong to the Lord yet have a disdain for people made in the image and likeness of God and Christ Jesus just like they are.

Further, the Bible is clear about apostasy in these last days, stating many shall fall away (2 Thessalonians 2:3). Many Pastors preach and teach on the rapture, like a forgone conclusion that this epidemic of heart disease in the church will somehow take care of itself or get overlooked like everything else we refuse to deal with and try to cover by grace. So, I ask, is the collective body of the church "there" as it professes? We should know we are not there yet by the massive amounts of people walking away from the faith and the church seeking worldly and practical wisdom and knowledge instead of God's life-giving wisdom. We also should know we are not there yet, witnessing a generation who have mostly rejected the holiness God in Christ Jesus requires for a gospel that emphasizes God allows everything through the world's definition of love. We know we are not there yet, witnessing the doctrines of demons that have gone unchecked and defiling many churches worldwide. Our Lord and Savior asked, "when the Son of Man comes, will He really find faith on the earth," (Luke 18:8)?

So, Brother Wash, where is "there"? "There" refers to a place in our spiritual walk where our conscience and minds can boldly go to the sweet feet of Christ Jesus and hear well done, my good and faithful servant (Matthew 25:21, 23). "There" refers to rest for your souls here in time while life and the enemy shoot fiery arrows at you or while you wait patiently on the Lord in eternity in your resting place (Revelation 6:11). "There," my friends, is the confidence knowing and keeping the three commands of Christ Jesus, which He stated 1) seek ye first, 2) the most important commandment, and 3) this one thing is necessary. The Holy Scriptures say,

- But seek first the Kingdom of God and His righteousness, and all these things shall be added to you (Matthew 6:33)

- Jesus answered him, "The first of all the commandments is: Hear, O Israel, the Lord our God, the Lord is one. And you shall love the Lord your God with all your heart, with all your soul, with all your mind, and with all your strength.' This is the first commandment. And the second, like it, is this: 'You shall love your neighbor as yourself.' There is no other commandment greater than these," (Mark 12:29-31).

- But the Lord answered and said to her, "Martha, Martha, you are worried and distracted by many things; but only one thing is necessary; for Mary has chosen the good part, which shall not be taken away from her," (Luke 10:41-42).

This knowledge is the difference between being confident, ignorant, or arrogant of your eternal reward at a critical time in the history of the world.

The Eighth Expose: Shall Live

"You shall live" describes the covenant relationship God has in Christ Jesus and, through the power of the Holy Spirit, with the chosen people called to reign in eternity with Him. Everyone will live somewhere after the expiration of their EARTH suit, but only the chosen shall live because of their covenantal relationship with Christ Jesus. There are two days you will never forget once you have learned why they are so crucial in the life of a believer. The first is your natural birthday. The Bible says while you were yet in your mother's womb, God has unique plans for you and that you have a purpose (Psalms 139:16-17). How many Believers ask the Lord what His plans are for their lives before they venture off on their own? The second date occurs at your baptism and acceptance of Christ Jesus as your Lord and Savior. Jesus said, "You must be reborn of water and Spirit to inherit the Kingdom of God," (John 3:3). We call this your RB2 date. These two dates are the most important in any Believer's life, the day you were born into this earth, and the day you were born into the spirit. This knowledge is a valuable tool when making disciples. Exposure to these two dates will help you never again stumble when confronted about your faith. The recognition alone that you have the dates written in your heart and mind shows a sincere motivation to be right in the sight of God. For most, this means you have genuinely realized the significance of spiritual rebirth for the professed Christians.

Things are bound to distract you and offend you in this life; that is inevitable. However, you need to get those two days defined in your life right now. When you left your mother's body, everything around you began to shape the plans He had for your life. Your purpose started there, and your clock started the second you exited your mother's womb.

The Ninth Expose: The Disclaimers

There is a method behind the process and a sure means to end this sin-filled world. We know humanity didn't listen to God and His prophets; they did not listen to Jesus and his prophets, and chances are humankind will not listen to the Holy Spirit and the words He has given me or other messengers like me the Lord has called (Jeremiah 6:10) to prepare the hearts of His people for his coming. God, all knowing, righteous, and just placed throughout His word disclaimers, completely exonerating Himself from the liabilities of humanity's wicked and deceitful heart. It is disheartening the things I see and hear daily, such as disregarding His existence, no realization of His power, and doubting the Word of God that will prove unprofitable to all who do not believe. "'All your idols, all your gold, silver, and bronze, let them save you,' says the Lord God of Hosts!" (Jeremiah 2:28). No man, government, religion, and anything other than the Lamb of God can save you from the hand of the Lord God of recompenses (Jeremiah 51:56) on the day of judgment. This disclaimer was good then and holds today as we are in the last days, most assuredly.

Many are the overlooked, misunderstood, and blatantly ignored disclaimers Christ Jesus gave us throughout His earthly ministry. The one I want to focus on, though, is the very last thing the angel of the Lord said to "whosoever wills," which means everybody. The Holy Scriptures says, "He that is unjust let him be unjust still; he, which is filthy, let him be filthy still; he that is righteous let him be righteous still, and he that is holy, let him be holy still," (Revelation 22:10). For many delusional and deceived Christians, this is the rope that will hang so many over the eternal fire. In a world where people do not want to know the truth because it's just easier to believe and live a lie, many will face judgment and want to blame God (Proverbs 19:3 NLT).

Finally, the most widely known and controversial disclaimer, mainly because of its eternal ramifications given by Christ Jesus, is blasphemy against the Holy Spirit. The Bible says, "But the blasphemy against the Holy Spirit will not be forgiven in this age or the next," (Matthew 12:31-32). Now that you have a defined and refined explanation of the Kingdom of God and have read Chapter Four, "No Fourth Option," you can clearly understand that there are no more chances, three is the magic number given in the Bible, before you can expect judgment (Amos 2:4). This generation is as close to the fulfillment of the Gentiles as any other time in history by the rate of lawlessness, violence, sorcery, and idolatry rapidly outpacing disciples being recruited (2 Timothy 3:13). This message of the Kingdom of God could be one of the last given before our Lord and Savior's return for His bride, the enduring Church. No one knows; therefore, we must continue to look up, watch and pray that we might be found worthy to stand before Christ Jesus blameless upon His return (Luke 21:36).

Envision the Promise Now to Him who is able to keep you from stumbling, and to present you faultless before the presence of His glory with exceeding joy, to God our Savior, Who alone is wise, Be glory and majesty, Dominion and power, Both now and forever, *(Jude 1:24-25).*

KAP IT III

"D.E.S. P.L.A.N.E."

"Because thou hast kept the word of my patience, I also will keep thee from the hour of temptation, which shall come upon all the world, to test them that dwell upon the earth" (Revelation 3:10). "No temptation has overtaken you, but such as is common to man, and God is faithful, who will not allow you to be tempted beyond what you are able, but with the temptation will provide the way of escape also so that you will be able to endure it," (1 Corinthians 10:13).

The First Expose: "DES PLANE"

The Holy Scriptures tell us no one knows the day or hour that the Son of Man will return (Matthew 24:36). However, we have insight into that time given through Christ Jesus and His holy prophets to prepare us for this series of monumental events. Jesus advised us on that day to look up when we see all these events taking place because His return is imminent (Luke 21:28). When we look up today, often, we will see an airplane or traces of one going across the sky. The KAP IT precept D.E.S. P.L.A.N.E. is derived from a popular T.V. show in the late 1970s called "Fantasy Island." Each show would begin with Herve' Villechaize ringing a bell, yelling, "the plane," "the plane"! There were two main characters, Mr. Rourke, played by Ricardo Montalban, the overseer, and Tattoo, his assistant. Each show had a host of celebrity guests flown to an exotic island, where they paid $50,000 for a weekend stay to get a fantasy reenacted and fulfilled. Like clockwork, the plane arrived and departed on time, and the guests always left with some new important revelation about their future life. As it is in the natural, so it is in the spiritual (McClure).

The Second Expose: "The "Divine Exit Strategy" (DES)

Our hope in these last days is that we who believe, trust, and obey will experience the same glorious exit our Lord and Savior Christ Jesus experienced in the presence of the eleven disciples. After completing His earthly ministry, including the ushering in of the Kingdom of God, presided by the Holy Spirit, Jesus then returned home to heaven as a new creation. He is the first of His kind and the prototype in which all humankind will follow suit in the age to come (Colossians 1:18). The Holy Scriptures tell us that we will also depart in a likewise manner, not to proceed those who have fallen asleep, to meet the Lord in the air (1 Thessalonians 4:15). The Lord, our God, always provides a means of escape for His people.

Wrath and condemnation are not the True Church's final destinations but partakers of salvation and eternal life. However, the Bible commands that we must watch and pray always to avoid the wrath and much more counted worthy to escape all the things that shall happen to the earth's inhabitants (Luke 21:36).

This adherence means we must not take for granted that we have made it because we have the covenant of Grace on our side, but continually humble ourselves before the Lord. This KAP IT precept coined the D.E.S. P.L.A.N.E. is encouragement for the believer in these challenging times. D.E.S. P.L.A.N.E. is an acronym meaning: The Devine Exit Strategy,

• Prophesied (1 Corinthians 15:50-57)

• Prepared (John 14:3)

• Permanent (Matthew 28:20)

• Leaving (time) (2 Corinthians 5:8)

• Living (1 Thessalonians 4)

• Arrangement (in) (1 Thessalonians 4:16)

• Eternity (Isaiah 57:15)

The Third Expose: The 144,000 X 2

The Book of Revelation mentions two sets of a hundred and forty-four thousand individuals who will serve God and Christ Jesus. God had twelve tribes; likewise, Jesus had twelve apostles that are holy unto Him. God has a hundred and forty-four thousand set aside from his twelve tribes and Jesus, as He always does, follows the model of His Father for His Kingdom, also having a hundred and forty-four thousand from the entire earth. These groups of individuals are holy, set apart, and special to God and the Lamb of God. The first set of a hundred and forty-four thousand have these attributes, and the purpose of the twelve tribes of Israel is as follows (Revelation 7:1-8).

• Servants of God (Revelation 7:3)

• The sealed children of Israel (Revelation 7:4)

• Only of the twelve tribes of Israel (Revelation 7:5)

• Twelve thousand individuals each from the twelve tribes (Revelation 7:5)

The second set of a hundred and forty-four thousand has these attributes and this purpose (Revelation 14:1). These men are

• Not defiled with women (Revelation 14:4)

• All virgins (Revelation 14:4)

- Blameless (Revelation 14:4)

- Redeemed of men (Revelation 14:4)

- No deceit in their mouth (Revelation 14:5)

- Without fault before the throne of God (Revelation 14:5)

- First Fruits to God and the Lamb (Revelation 14:4)

- Follow the Lamb wherever He goes (Revelation 14:4)

First Class Marriage Supper of the Lamb. (Rapture)

In heaven, located in the Book of Life, is a list of individuals established before the earth's foundations that received the promise of eternal life. For this work, we call it CLASS, which stands for the (Consolidated List of Assimilated Sanctified Saints). On three differing and separate events, 1) the Marriage Supper of the Lamb, 2) the First Resurrection, and 3) the White Throne Judgment, these three differing PLANES will come to deliver the saints, prophets, servants of Christ Jesus and the world as well to their home where he is or their final resting place (Revelation 20:1-6).

The first CLASS includes the following attributes to avoid tribulation (Thessalonians 5:9).

<u>Marriage Supper of the Lamb</u>

- Made of The Overcoming Church (Revelation 3:12)

- Endured Patiently (Revelation 3:10)

- Had the Holy Spirit, Witness to Jesus
  (1 Corinthians 6:9)

- They held on to their belief in the Word of God
  (Revelation 3:8)

- Did not worship the beast (Revelation 13:15)

- Did not attain the beast image (Revelation 13:15)

- Did not receive the mark of the beast in their hand
  (Revelation 13:16)

- Did not receive the mark of the beast on their
  forehead and will avoid tribulation (Revelation 13:16)

- Will reign 1000 years with Jesus as Priest in His
  Kingdom (Revelation 20:6)

- Will face judgment for their reward, not
  condemnation (Revelation 20:4)

Second Class: *The First Resurrection*

A second group (Consolidated List of Assimilated Sanctified
Saints) will depart to make their home with the Lord after the
tribulation. Once revealed, the beast will command all to
worship him or die during the tribulation. Those remaining

on earth will choose to keep the commandments of God and the faith of Jesus or follow the likeness and image of the beast. The Believers who patiently endure will consist of

- Martyred Saints (Revelation 6:9)

- Did not worship the beast or his image (Revelation 20:4)

- Did not receive his mark on their foreheads or hands

- Have the Holy Spirit and the witness to Jesus (Acts 5:32)

- Cling to their belief in the Word of God (Revelation 12:11)

- Reigned with Christ Jesus one thousand years Everyone not raised in the First Resurrection has an extended dirt nap of one thousand years (Revelation 20:5)

- Will face judgment (Revelation 20:12)

- Blessed and Holy (Revelation 20:6)

- Priest of God and Christ Jesus (Revelation 20:6)

- Not affected by the Second Death (Revelation 20:6)

The Third Expose: Great White Throne Judgment

This PLANE is for the world and everybody who has not left on one of the first two planes. The earth and the heavens are gone, burnt up, and there is only one place you can go: on your knees to face the only True God of the universe on His throne. At His right hand is the Son of Man, the Son of God who is King, judge, and ruler of heaven and earth. The Bible says every entity containing souls will give up its dead for judgment; the sea, the earth, hell, and the grave will all have to give up their occupants for eternal judgment.

Great White Throne Judgment

If anyone's name doesn't appear in the Lamb's Book of Life, he will be cast into the S.P.A. (Satan's Permanent Abode), the lake of fire (Revelation 20:10)

- The beast
- The false prophet
- The devil
- Death
- Hades
- Everyone not written in the Book of Life

The Fourth Expose: NICHE

The challenge of this generation to shed this life and seek a more fulfilling life beyond this EARTH suit is complicated and borderline impossible for some because of fear and disbelief. As stated before, humankind is visually motivated and primarily stimulated through our addictions to comfort and pleasure. So how can a natural man be convinced by the Bible that tells us to be poor with reverence for God is more rewarding than being rich (Luke 20-24)?

Similarly, how does the natural man somehow believe that the death of a consecrated body dedicated to the Lord will raise a glorified body? For those chosen, we can look forward to an incredible existence lasting forever with our Lord and Savior, Christ Jesus, in His new position as King of Heaven and earth. We also benefit by inheriting the same body He now possesses as the first creation and firstborn from the dead. The hope of the True Believer is the promise of eternal life coupled with the commitment to a new body devoid of decay. We encourage each other by faith in Christ Jesus alone, our redeemer, and our belief in the Holy Scriptures through a great set of witnesses. Deceived by so many dead, unspiritual, and unprofitable things, it is almost impossible for the world to grasp the message of the Gospel and partake of the glorious new life and body (NICHE) that God has planned for those who love Him, do not love their lives to the death and keep the commandments of His only begotten Son Christ Jesus (Revelation 12:11).

The flip side is, sadly, some will be amongst the unbelieving and dead in Christ Jesus, who will also inherit a type of glorified body. This body, however, will not live with Christ Jesus where He is, nor will it inherit the gift of salvation but rather a condemnation. The glorified body of the unbeliever will be subject to excruciating anguish in fire forever and ever (Revelation 20:15). So don't play Russian roulette with your eternity because no one can afford to lose.

Envision the Promise "In my Father's house are many mansions: if it were not so, I would have told you. I go to prepare a place for you. And if I go and prepare a place for you, I will come again, and receive you unto myself; that where I am, there ye may be also," (John 14:1-2).

REFERENCES

American Worldview Inventory, Arizona Christian
University & Barna, . *The World's Most Shocking
Church Statistics.* 2020.
https://igniteamerica.com/ignite-shocking-stats/. 14
April 2023.

Bible IQ. "5 Reasons Why the Bible is the Most Important
Book on Earth." 11 April 2023. *Bible !Q.*
https://www.bibleiq.org/5-reasons-why-the-bible-is-
the-most-important-book-on-earth/. 11 April 2023.

Birkbeck, Tim. *Preachers use YouTube to spread their
message far and wide.* 18 October 2019.
https://www.basingstokegazette.co.uk/news/179759
31.preachers-use-youtube-spread-message-far-
wide/. 13 April 2023.

Christian Classics Ethereal Library. *Apostlels Creed.* 2015
March 2015.
https://www.ccel.org/creeds/apostles.creed.html. 13
April 2023.

Johns, Logan. *Timeline of the End Times The Cross
Pentecost Church Age Rapture 7 Years 3 ½ Second
Coming Millennium 1,000 Years Eternity.* 10 June
2016. https://slideplayer.com/slide/5759686/. 10
June 2023.

Kaneda, Toshiko, and Carl Haub. *How Many People Have
Ever Lived on Earth?* 15 November 2022.
https://www.prb.org/articles/how-many-people-
have-ever-lived-on-earth/. 13 April 2022.

McClure, Dena. *The Coming Glory:As It Is In The Natural
So it Is In the Spiritual.* 29 October 2012.
http://denamcclure.com/all-posts/the-coming-glory-
as-it-is-in-the-natural-so-it-is-in-the-spiritual/. 14
April 2023.

National Fatherhood Initiative. *The Statistics Don't Lie:
Fathers Matter.* 3 April 2022.

https://www.fatherhood.org/father-absence-statistic. 3 APRIL 2023.

National Geographic Society. *How Did Scientists Calculate the Age of Earth?* 2 June 2022. www.nationalgeographic.org,. 1 APRIL 2023.

Nelson, Thomas. *Find It Fast In The Bible: The Ultimate A to Z Resource* . Nashville: Thomas Nelson Publishers, 2000.

Numerology Center. *Bibical Numerology Number 3*. 12 April 2023. http://numerology.center/biblical_numbers_number _3.php. 12 April 2023.

Pew Research Center. *When Americans Say They Believe in God, What Do They Mean?* 25 April 2018. https://www.pewresearch.org/religion/2018/04/25/w hen-americans-say-they-believe-in-god-what-do-they-mean/. 1 April 2023.

The Bible Sojourner. *What Was the Population of Earth Before the Flood?* 12 February 2022. https://petergoeman.com/population-earth-flood/. 4 April 2023.

Toledo, Chelsea, and Kirstie Saltsman. *Genetics by the Numbers*. 12 June 2012. https://nigms.nih.gov/education/Inside-Life-Science/Pages/Genetics-by-the-Numbers.aspx#:~:text=The%20DNA%20of%20any %20two,also%20contributes%20to%20our%20indi viduality. 13 April 2023.

ACKNOWLEDGMENTS

First, honoring God, in Christ Jesus, and the power of the Holy Spirit for His faithfulness and love toward me, His servant!

With special thanks:

To my publisher, editor, friend, Dr. Sonia Leverette, and the entire Hadassah's Crown Publishing family, I am incredibly indebted to you for sticking with me during this long process. Thank you for your prayers, all the time, and patience!

To my editor, Sis Petals Hood, for your extraordinary diligence, focus, and time management in helping me complete this good work.

To my graphic designer and computer guru, Surge Tech, for being there and providing excellent service when I needed it most!

To Mary, my kids: Sha'Keela, Justin, Keshawn, and Logan, I love and thank you all for encouraging me through all up and the down times.

To my immediate family for providing all the content; I could ever need to write a book this relevant and revealing.

To the countless people, God used to interact with me throughout my life to expose, empty, provoke, and encourage me in this writing process.

To the Carlsons, Stan & Ruth, my sister in Christ, Cyndi Sublette, and my BnB family praise the Lord! Thank you for taking me into your Texas home and providing me with such a beautiful and God-fearing atmosphere to get a lot of work done. God bless you and all connected to you and your entire family.

To Brother Hao Wu and his dad of Wu Ministries, who God used to get me in a quiet place so that I could genuinely hear a word from Him who loved and saved me to complete this good work! Thank you, and God bless you, my brothers!

CONTACTING THE AUTHOR

This is the first of several books to be published by the author. He can be contacted at **browash@odaatm456.live**

Made in the USA
Columbia, SC
20 July 2023

20583697R00191